D1708040

PRINCIPLES
OF
PASSIVE SOLAR BUILDING DESIGN
With Microcomputer Programs

Pergamon Titles of Related Interest

ALAWI *et al.*	Solar Energy and the Arab World
COWAN	Predictive Methods for the Energy Conservation of Buildings
FERRARO *et al.*	Monitoring Solar Heating Systems: A Practical Handbook
HOWELL	Your Solar Energy Home: Including Wind and Methane Applications
ISFALT	Energy Saving Building Design
JAGER	Solar Energy Applications in Houses
JANZEN and SWARTMAN	Solar Energy Conversion II
McVEIGH	Sun Power: An Introduction to the Applications of Solar Energy, 2nd Edition
STONE	Building Economy, 3rd Edition
YANNAS	Passive and Low Energy Architecture

Related Journals

Sample copies available on request

Civil Engineering for Practicing and Design Engineers

Energy

Energy Conversion and Management

International Journal of Forensic Engineering

Journal of Heat Recovery Systems

Mathematical Modelling

Solar and Wind Technology

Solar Energy

Software

IBM-compatible software covering the programs in this text is available on 5¼ inch floppy disc, DOS 2.X. For more details, write to: Johan De Villiers Architect, R.R. No. 3 [Sherbrook St. West], Peterborough, Ontario K9J 6X4, Canada.

PRINCIPLES
OF
PASSIVE SOLAR BUILDING DESIGN
With Microcomputer Programs

CYRIL CARTER
Environmental Resource and Studies Program,
Trent University, Ontario

and

JOHAN DE VILLIERS
Johan De Villiers Architect,
Ontario

PERGAMON PRESS
NEW YORK · OXFORD · BEIJING · FRANKFURT
SÃO PAULO · SYDNEY · TOKYO · TORONTO

721.0467
C 32 p

U.S.A.	Pergamon Press, Maxwell House, Fairview Park, Elmsford, New York 10523, U.S.A.
U.K.	Pergamon Press, Headington Hill Hall, Oxford OX3 0BW, England
PEOPLE'S REPUBLIC OF CHINA	Pergamon Press, Room 4037, Qianmen Hotel, Beijing, People's Republic of China
FEDERAL REPUBLIC OF GERMANY	Pergamon Press, Hammerweg 6, D-6242 Kronberg, Federal Republic of Germany
BRAZIL	Pergamon Editora, Rua Eça de Queiros, 346, CEP 04011, Paraiso, São Paulo, Brazil
AUSTRALIA	Pergamon Press Australia, P.O. Box 544, Potts Point, N.S.W. 2011, Australia
JAPAN	Pergamon Press, 8th Floor, Matsuoka Central Building, 1-7-1 Nishishinjuku, Shinjuku-ku, Tokyo 160, Japan
CANADA	Pergamon Press Canada, Suite No. 271, 253 College Street, Toronto, Ontario, Canada M5T 1R5

Copyright © 1987 Pergamon Books Inc.

All Rights Reserved. No part of this publication may be reproduced, stored in a retrieval system or transmitted in any form or by any means: electronic, electrostatic, magnetic tape, mechanical, photocopying, recording or otherwise, without permission in writing from the publishers.

First printing 1987

Library of Congress Cataloging in Publication Data
Carter, Cyril.
Principles of passive solar building design.
Bibliography: p.
Includes index.
1. Solar houses—Design and construction.
2. Solar energy—Passive systems. 3. Solar energy—
Data processing. I. De Villiers, Johan. II. Title.
TH7414.C39   1987   721'.0467   86–25133
ISBN 0-08-033637-X Hardover
ISBN 0-08-033636-1 Flexicover

Printed in Great Britain by A. Wheaton & Co. Ltd., Exeter

Contents

UNIVERSITY LIBRARIES
CARNEGIE-MELLON UNIVERSITY
PITTSBURGH, PENNSYLVANIA 15213

Preface and Acknowledgements

This book is primarily intended for architecture and engineering professionals who design buildings, but much of it should be accessible to the interested layman. *Principles of Passive Solar Building Design* covers all types of design in which the building itself acts as a solar collector, with or without the use of fans to move heated air through the building. Passive design has a very long history, but recent interest dates from the 1973 oil crisis. Energy saving is an important part of passive design, but it is not the only factor, and the authors believe it has been overemphasised in many recent publications. Six years ago, one of the authors replaced a small window in his own living room with a large window covering most of the south wall. This was done primarily to capture solar energy, but it also produced a delightful integration of living room and garden. Passive solar design can save energy and create better living spaces.

Some of the interest in passive solar design has been superseded recently by an enthusiasm for "energy-efficient" building design. Symptomatic of this is the decision of the American magazine *Solar Age* to change its name to *Progressive Builder*. In writing this book, the authors are trying to resist this trend. While recognizing the importance of nonsolar energy-efficient building design, we believe that solar design is still vital, and assisted by appropriate design aids, offers many opportunities for innovative designers.

The book is divided into two main parts, on the qualitative principles of passive design and the quantitative aspects of predicting temperature variations and energy performance. This follows the model set by the U.S. Department of Energy *Passive Solar Design Handbook* in 1980, but our quantitative section is oriented to the use of microcomputer design aids. It aims to encourage innovative design with flexible computer programs that stay as close as possible to the basic physical principles of heat transfer.

One somewhat facetious critic of the Department of Energy handbook said that Part 1 contained all that we already knew, whereas Part 2 contained all that we would never want to know. We have obviously left ourselves open to the same sort of comment, but we have consciously tried hard to avoid this trap. Inevitably, the seasoned solar designer may not get much new from Part 1, but we hope the book will be read by many building designers who have not previously given much thought to solar design.

The book also contains tables of weather data from around the world. We wish to thank the Atmospheric Service of Environment Canada for helping with the compilation of these data from various sources. Our thanks also to Yair Zarmi of the Solar Research Institute of the University of the Negev, who read the complete manuscript and offered valuable comments. A succession of student research assistants helped write the computer programs, prepare the drawings, and check the manuscript. Thanks to Cynthia Brown, Joan Tickle, Peter Hughes, Darryl Freitag, Pam Martin, Francine Cann, Wendi Scholfield, and Ian Gatensby, and to Taru Freeman, who helped put the early drafts of the book onto the word processor. Financial support for research was provided by the Natural Sciences and Engineering Research Council of Canada and Canada Mortgage and Housing Corporation. The Ontario Ministry of Energy provided funding for the construction of a super-solar demonstration building, which the authors used to clarify their ideas on some aspects of passive design. Some of the computer programs were developed in 1983 when Carter was an NSERC Senior Industrial Fellow with Spectrum Engineering Company. Colleagues in the Solar Energy Society of Canada provided continual stimulation. Any errors remaining are the responsibility of the authors, and we would appreciate hearing about them.

PRINCIPLES
OF
PASSIVE SOLAR BUILDING DESIGN

With Microcomputer Programs

Introduction

While governments and business search for new energy sources, the sun continues to send out vast amounts of high quality energy. Although only 1 trillionth of this energy reaches the Earth, this is still about 10,000 times the total commercial energy used, so that even very modest progress in utilising solar energy could provide us with a large part of our energy needs. On a clear day, a surface directly facing the sun receives about 1 kW of solar radiation per square meter. Only about one tenth of this is received on a cloudy day and, of course, there is none at all at night. On average, much of the populated world receives 200 W/m^2 of solar radiation.

A great deal of research is being conducted into methods of utilising this abundant but rather diffuse and spasmodic source of energy. One of the currently most effective methods is to admit the sunshine into buildings through glazed apertures, and to utilise the solar energy for space and water heating, largely through clever building design, rather than elaborate mechanical equipment. Such building design has become known as *passive solar*.

Passive solar creates images of tanned bodies lazing in the sun. To some, perhaps, it carries indolent, or even decadent, connotations, inappropriate in a get-ahead technological society. Although some passive solar enthusiasts may want to escape from modern society, one does not have to take this approach in order to appreciate the possible advantages of using the sun's energy to replace oil, gas, or nuclear power.

In some ways the term passive solar is unfortunate, because it suggests that no mechanical aids should be allowed. Most passive solar designs, in fact, put the emphasis more on the building itself being the solar collector, rather than on the complete absence of pumps or fans; so passive solar design might more appropriately be called integrated solar design. However, the term passive solar is now so widely used that it would be futile to try to change it.

Passive solar design is the attempt to satisfy the building occupants' needs for space, heating, cooling, and lighting as far as possible by natural means, using the building design itself to collect and store solar energy when it is needed, to exclude solar energy when it is not needed, and to encourage natural cooling. Building design incorporates not just the building but the local environment as well. Some authors have called it "designing with nature" or "designing with climate," and often stress the fact that much of it is a return to traditional building methods. Without our modern methods for heating, lighting, and cooling, our ancestors were forced to design with nature. If all that was now required was a return to the "good old days," there would be no need to write a book about passive solar design, or about anything else for that matter. The authors have seen too many poorly conceived attempts to utilise passive solar energy to ascribe to this view.

Passive solar design at its best is the integration of the architect's aesthetic endeavour to create interesting and satisfying living spaces with the basic scientific and engineering principles of solar radiation, heat transfer, and air circulation. The two authors of this book, a practicing architect and an applied mathematician, represent the two principal themes.

Much of the writings on passive solar design have been overly concerned with the energy savings aspects, which has led some designers inexorably in the direction of the tightly sealed box, with minimal window area. Such buildings can be heated mostly by their own internal heat gains, from people and heat-generating appliances. In some ways, these buildings were a reaction against the mistakes and insupportable claims of some of the more ardent solar enthusiasts, but they leave out the less tangible aspects of our relationship with the sun.

Life on Earth is basically a product of the sun, and retains a mystical relationship with it. Man no longer worships the sun as a god, as our ancestors did, but the annual pilgrimage to the "Sunbelt" in search of the tan that signifies salvation shows that sun worship is far from dead. There is no doubt that appropriate amounts of sunshine are good for the human spirit. Passive solar design must take account of this factor as well as the gigajoules of energy saved.

Roland Edward Rouse has written[1]:

> If we can cut energy use so low with conservation, . . . why should we bother with passive solar? The reason is simple. Passive solar features sell buildings. They produce qualities that energy conservation cannot. Climate-adapted design not only saves heat. It helps make better buildings, buildings that people like. Conservation principles suggest fewer windows, but most consumers think otherwise. Reduced glass cuts heat loss at the expense of other values, including solar heat, visual comfort, and the quality of the indoor environment.

Fanis Grammenos[2] of the Canadian Mortgage Housing Corporation has also called for a reversal of the recent trend towards smaller windows, and has stressed the importance of sunlight in maintaining both physical and psychological health.

This book aims to outline the basic principles of passive solar design and to offer some simple quantitative design aids that could stimulate innovative passive designs.

[1]Roland Edward Rouse, A developer's guide to multifamily passive housing. *Solar Age* **8**(10), 23–27 (1983).

[2]Fanis Grammenos, Canadian Mortgage and Housing Corporation, Ottawa, in an unpublished article sent to the authors: Light, health, and passive solar design.

PART 1

Qualitative Principles

CHAPTER 1

Site and Climate

SUBDIVISION AND SITE LAYOUT

An ideal site for a passive solar building has unimpeded access to sunshine during the winter heating season and is protected from cold winter winds by the natural contours of the ground or by evergreen vegetation or both. It is shaded from unneeded summer sunshine by deciduous vegetation and other means. A site that slopes to the south in the northern hemisphere, or to the north in the southern hemisphere often makes it easier to satisfy these requirements. In rural areas, suitable sites can be chosen after a careful search. In built-up areas, careful planning and subdivision layout is necessary both in the initial building stages and also later to protect it from undesirable encroachments.

Subdivision layout can also significantly lower summer cooling requirements. For this purpose, there should be many properly placed trees, and a minimum area of black tarmac surfaces. The diagrams in Figures 1.1–1.3 by Canadian architect John Hix[3] illustrate how the same subdivision site can be laid out in alternative ways.

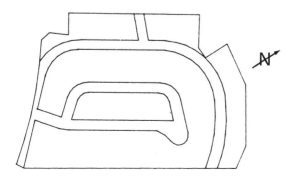

FIG. 1.1. Conventional site layout

---

[3]Figures 1.1–1.3 are based upon *Subdivisions and the Sun*. Ontario Government Bookstore, Toronto, Ontario, M5S 1Z8, 1979.

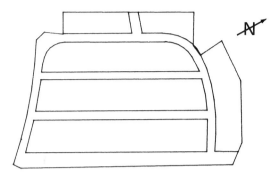

FIG. 1.2. Reasonable passive solar layout

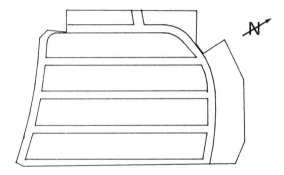

FIG. 1.3. Good passive solar layout

Each layout has 20 dwellings per hectare (8 per acre), which in practice would be a mixture of townhouses, detached, and semidetached houses. Passive solar design is straightforward on the third type, somewhat of a problem on the second, and difficult on the first. The first diagram (Figure 1.1) has conventional 20–21 m road widths and lot depths of 34 m. Lots are divided about equally between north entry on E–W streets, south entry on E–W streets, and N–S streets.

The second layout (Figure 1.2) retains conventional road widths and lot depths, but most of the lots are now on east–west streets. The third layout (Figure 1.3) reduces road widths to 17 m and lot depths to 26 m. Correspondingly, lot frontage is increased by 25%, thus increasing the potential solar gain area, and making it easier to accommodate garages and entrances on south entry lots.

Another possible solution is to eliminate south entry lots, by providing narrow E–W access lanes between lots, but this may raise extra problems in snow clearing and fire protection.

John Hix's study shows that the layout of Figure 1.3 allows about twice as much south-facing window area as the more conventional layout of Figure 1.1.

The general principle of solar access is that the sun's noon angle with the vertical is the latitude plus 23° in midwinter, and the latitude less 23° in midsummer. Thus at 45° latitude, the noon midwinter sun is 68° from vertical or 22° above the horizon. Any obstacle below 22° will block the sun from a solar collector or window for part of the day. The sunpath chart section at the end of the book describes how sun charts may be used to assess the effect of obstructions on the collection of solar energy.

The legal aspects of protecting solar access have been considered in many jurisdictions, and some progress has been made. Generally, however, solar access is best protected by good zoning bylaws and site layout, rather than by attempts to define "rights to sunshine." If the building is set on the north side of the site (in the northern hemisphere), then not only is the possibility of encroachment on solar access reduced, but the large sun-facing windows will be looking out on the garden.

Figure 1.4 shows a possible site layout for a small passive solar house. This layout satisfies all the requirements for winter screening and summer shading mentioned previously. The actual layout must be fitted to the site, depending on elevations, desirable (or undesirable) views, neighbouring buildings, and so on.

LANDSCAPING OF SITE

Landscaping involves the deliberate change of the contours of the ground, and the planting of trees and other vegetation, as in Figure 1.5. This is normally done on any site to make it more attractive visually, but it can also play a major role in protecting the building from cold winter winds and shading out the hot summer sun. If the site does not have a natural sun-facing slope, some of the advantages of such a slope can be injected by berming the earth around the north side of the building. This not only provides extra protection from winds, but also adds extra insulation.

In the northern hemisphere, large evergreen trees or shrubbery planted on the north and northwest side of the site can often provide valuable wind protection without affecting solar access. In urban areas, it is important to remember that the north side of one site may be the south side of a neighbouring site. On the solar side of the site, between southeast and southwest in the northern hemisphere, deciduous trees can provide shading in the summer, but the trees need to be selected with care. Some trees with thick branches may screen out much of the winter sun if they are badly placed, and others retain their leaves so late into the autumn that they block out the sun when it could provide useful heat.

Table 1.1[4] gives sun-penetration and wind-modifying characteristics of some common trees. Trees also provide a lowering of the summer local ambient temperature as moisture evaporates from the leaves. Vines or climbing plants on the outside walls of buildings can reduce summer solar gain, particularly on east and west walls, and can also provide some screening from winter winds.

EFFECT OF CLIMATE

Passive solar design has something to offer in nearly all climates, but obviously the requirements vary. Most locations outside the tropics have some sort of winter season when ambient temperatures drop below comfort levels. If there is substantial winter sunshine, good design can capture, retain, and utilise that solar energy. If the winter is often overcast, ambient temperatures are usually not too extreme and diffuse sunlight may be useful. If the winter is both cloudy and cold, superinsulation and sealing techniques may still make it possible to supply most of a building's heating requirements from the normal internal heat gains.

In some locations, summer cooling may be more important than winter heating. Clearly, the large amounts of summer solar energy may potentially be used to drive mechanical cooling devices; this potential is being actively researched and developed.

---

[4]Table 1.1 is adapted from a study by M. M. Dillon Ltd., also reported in *Subdivisions and the Sun* (Note 3).

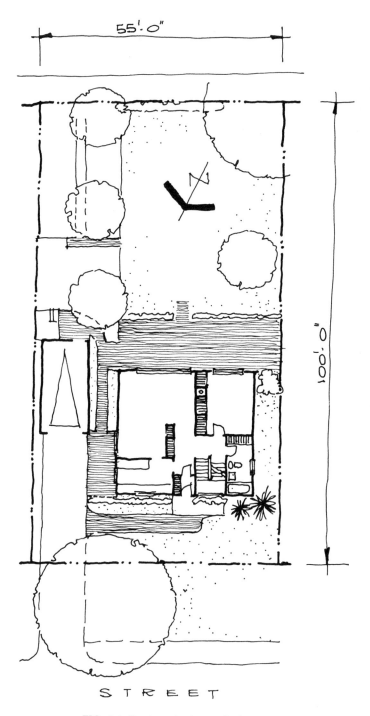

FIG. 1.4. Passive solar house site layout

As with active solar heating devices, however, active solar cooling will only make sense after all passive design measures have been incorporated into the building.

The first essential of passive cooling design is to keep as much as possible of unwanted solar and internal heat gain out of the building. The importance of sun-

FIG. 1.5. Well-landscaped passive solar house

shading has already been discussed, and most people in warm summer locations have long recognised the desirability of relaxing and cooking outside the building. If there is a substantial temperature difference between day and night, then opening of windows at night, possibly with the use of fans, is a useful strategy. Unfortunately, security requirements have destroyed this option in many commercial and some residential buildings, and some other method of night ventilation may be needed.

Air movement can make warm temperatures more comfortable, and the use of fans to achieve this is a well-established technique. Good passive design can stimulate air movement in a building by natural convection without the use of fans. The main effect of the air movement is to evaporate moisture from the skin. The latent heat required for evaporation is taken from the body, with a subsequent cooling effect. If the air is very humid, this evaporation process is more difficult, and the comforting effect of air movement is reduced. Hence, in climates with warm humid summers, moisture generation within the building should be minimised and windows kept closed during the day.

Summer breezes can provide a significant cooling effect if they are properly directed by good site and building design. Winter winds, however, can devastate the thermal behaviour of an exposed building. They can penetrate small cracks in the building envelope and increase the surface heat loss from walls and roofs.

Snow accumulation can be both an asset and a liability. Snow can provide extra insulation on flat or low slope roofs and can reflect extra solar radiation onto sun-facing windows. It can, however, accumulate on or near inclined windows or solar collectors, which not only blocks off useful sunshine but may also cause water leaks at the lower window seal.

Modern designers can learn much about "designing with climate" from traditional indigenous architecture in many parts of the world as described, for example, by Ken Butti and John Perlin.[5] The beneficial use of thick adobe walls by the Aztecs in Mexico has been recognized by many architects in the southern United States. The malqaf, or windcatch, is a shaft rising high above the building with a windward opening. It was used by the ancient Egyptians as long ago as 1300 B.C. and further developed in many hot arid areas of the Arab world.

[5]Ken Butti and John Perlin, *The Golden Thread*. Boyas, Boston, 1980.

TABLE 1.1. Trees for Winter Sun Penetration and Wind Modification*

Species	Sun	Wind break	Characteristics and comments	Height (m)	Growth rate	Form
Ash, European	P		Coarse branching habit	9–12	medium	small oval
white	G		Narrow, pyramidal crown	22–25	slow–medium	erect oval
Aspen, trembling	G		Open branching habit. Shallow, wide spreading roots; high debris production	16–21	rapid	narrow
Basswood	G		Slender ascending branch habit	22–25	medium–rapid	long oval
Beech, American	M		Keeps some leaves through winter	22–25	slow–medium	broad oval
Birch, white	G		Open, fine branching habit	15–22	medium–rapid	ascending
Butternut	G		Large, spreading crown, ascending branches. High debris production; low tolerance of salt	12–19	slow	irregular
Catalpa	P		Coarse branching habit, very dense foliage. High debris production; low resistance to disease	12–22	slow	irregular
Cedar, white	M		Dense branching habit and foliage	6–12	slow	dense conical
Cherry, choke	P	yes	Dense branching habit to ground. Good wildlife planting	8	medium–rapid	narrow irregular
Fir, balsam	M		Dense branching habit and foliage to ground. Shallow roots; low tolerance of salt	12–19	medium	conical
Ginkgo	G		Open, ascending branching habit. High debris production; low tolerance of disease	12–25	slow–medium	narrow oval
Hawthorn	P		Shrubby, retains berries through winter. High debris production. Thorns	2–6	slow–medium	broad
Hemlock, eastern	M		Dense foliage and branching habit. Shallow wide-spreading roots	9–22	slow	narrow conical
Hickory, shagbark	G		Open, coarse branching habit	12–25	slow	spreading
Horse chestnut	G		Coarse branching habit. High debris production; dense foliage	12–19	medium	stout oval
Larch	G		Loose open branching habit. Shallow, widespreading roots; high soil moisture	12–25	rapid	irregular, conical
Locust, honey	G		Open branching habit. Fine foliage, grows well in all soils	12–25	medium	irregular
Maple, Norway	G	yes	Fine branching habit. Dense foliage	12–22	rapid	rounded
red	P	yes	Ascending branches form a deep dense crown. Shallow roots	16–22	medium–rapid	broad oval
silver	G	yes	Loose open branching habit. Shallow roots	19–25	rapid	irregular
sugar	P	yes	Round topped crown, short branches	19–25	slow	oval ascending
Mountain ash	P		Open branches, retains berries through winter. High debris production	6–12	medium	spreading, oval
Oak, English	M		Holds onto some leaves during winter	6–25	slow–medium	oval conical
red	P		Coarse branching habit; holds some leaves in winter. Fastest growing oak	19–22	medium	elliptical
white	P		Wide spreading coarse branches	19–31	slow	elliptical
Pine, jack	M	yes	Ascending branches, open crown. High debris production	22–25	rapid	open, conical
red	M		Dense branching habit and foliage. Low tolerance of salt	16–25	medium	rounded conical
Scotch	M	yes	Open branching habit. High debris production; low tolerance of disease	12–25	rapid	irregular, conical
Poplar, Lombardy	P	yes	Branches to ground	16–22	rapid	narrow elliptical
Spruce, blue	M	yes	Dense branching habit and foliage. Low tolerance of salt	9–16	slow medium	dense pyramid
Walnut, black	P		Ascending wide spreading coarse branches	9–12	slow medium	wide spreading
Willow	P		Shrubby, fine branching habit. High debris production; shallow roots	12–16	rapid	irregular, drooping

*Winter sun penetration: good – G; partial – P; minimal – M

HUMAN COMFORT

Human comfort depends mainly on the ease with which the body can maintain a normal body temperature of 37°C. When not involved in strenuous physical activity, a human body continuously produces 100 to 150 W of heat. The ease with which this heat can be emitted to maintain comfort depends not only on the air temperature, but also on humidity, air movement, and heat radiation. In winter, a lower air temperature will be acceptable if humidity levels are not too low, air movement is reduced, and heat radiation impinges on the body. In summer, exactly the opposite behaviour of these three parameters is needed to make higher air temperatures acceptable.

It should be particularly noted that any design that maintains the building inside surfaces at a reasonable temperature will improve winter radiation comfort and permit air temperatures to be correspondingly lower.

Different people also have different comfort levels, based on their individual physiology, psychology, experience, and life-style. The ultimate test of a building's performance is not decided by computer simulations or physical measurements, but by the reactions of the building's occupants.

CHAPTER 2

Building Design, Sealing, Insulation

BUILDING SHAPE AND ORIENTATION

A building has minimum heat loss for a given floor area if it is square. However, good passive solar design requires it to be rectangular, with the long sides facing south and north, in order to maximise winter solar collection. Actually, a rectangle with sides in the ratio 3:2 has only 2% more heat loss than a square, so the two requirements are not seriously in conflict. Potential solar collection can be further increased if the southern face (in the northern hemisphere) is made taller than the northern face. This can be achieved either by a lower ground level or a higher roof level on the sunny side.

Shapes other than rectangular may be appropriate in certain circumstances. One well-known North American passive solar house[6] is L-shaped (Figure 2.1) with a glazed south-facing sun space inside the arms of the L. This makes it easy for the solar energy collected in the sun space to be distributed to the living spaces. The general principle remains, however, that a rectangular shape is more energy efficient, and should only be departed from if there is some specific reason.

The location of indoor spaces within the building deserves some attention. Bedrooms on the east receive the morning sun. Spaces such as garages, closets, stairs, hallways, bathrooms, and workshops, which are infrequently used, can conveniently be placed on the polar side of the building where they can act as a buffer between the main living areas and the outside.

AIR–VAPOUR BARRIERS AND SEALING

The importance of a good impervious and continuous air–vapour barrier has only recently become widely recognised. The general principle is that air carrying water vapour from the building interior must be prevented from seeping into the building

---

[6]This is the Balcomb house at First Village, Santa Fe, New Mexico.

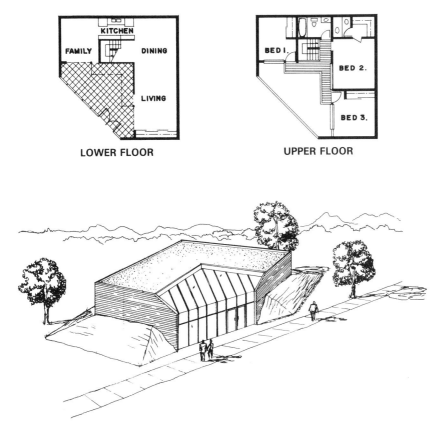

FIG. 2.1. L-shaped house plan

structure, where it would condense, possibly freeze, and damage the structure and insulation. The inside surface of the building must be made as impervious to moisture as possible, while the outside surface should be slightly leaky to allow any small amounts of moisture that may penetrate the barrier to escape. The techniques of air–vapour barrier installation lie outside the realm of design, and will not be discussed, but any building designer should ensure that the builder is familiar with these techniques. In the mid-1980s there is still some controversy about air–vapour barrier installation. Although some builders use thick polyethylene with caulked overlapped joints, others insist that appropriately sealed drywall can do the job more effectively and cheaply.[7]

A good air-vapour barrier is more important in locations with cold winters, but is desirable in any climate. Combined with a good barrier should be attention to the sealing of all openings in the barrier, chiefly around windows and doors, but also all those other smaller openings that may easily be overlooked (Figure 2.2). This combination of sealing and air–vapour barrier not only inhibits the undesirable movement of vapour, but also reduces air infiltration, which may be the principal heat-loss mechanism in a well-insulated building.

---

[7]Joseph Lstiburek is the principal advocate of airtight drywall. See *Solar Age* **11**(2), 7 (1986) for a brief discussion.

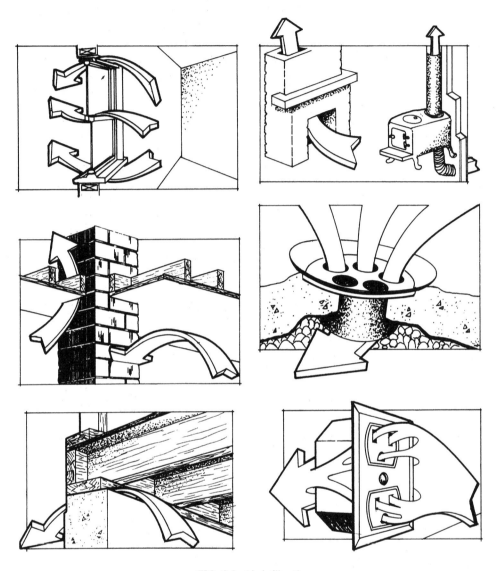

FIG. 2.2. Air infiltration

With very careful attention to detail, it is possible to make a building so tight that air to support combustion in furnaces and stoves may be inadequate, and air inside the building may become dangerously polluted. In this case it is desirable to provide an extra channel for combustion air and possibly controlled air infiltration with a fan or through an air-to-air heat exchanger, which recovers some of the heat content of the warm air leaving the building. The vapour barrier itself will provide some protection from radon gas emanating from the building materials, but will of course make it difficult for pollution generated inside the building to escape.

Passive solar design, as distinct from superinsulated building design, usually puts less emphasis on reducing air infiltration to these possibly dangerous levels and more emphasis on utilising and enjoying solar energy. As long as air infiltration is not reduced much below 0.5 air changes per hour, and some care is taken to minimise interior-generated pollution, a heat exchanger is not necessary, but mechanically controlled ventilation may be desirable.

Whether to install a heat exchanger or not is mainly an economic decision. Overall, after allowing for the remnant uncontrolled infiltration, and the losses in the exchanger, a heat exchanger can recover perhaps half of the heat content of the warm air leaving the building. The exchanger's capital cost needs to be justified on the basis of the value of the heat saved.

AIR INFILTRATION MEASUREMENT

Air infiltration into a building is checked and measured by a depressurisation device called an infiltrometer. This reduces the pressure inside the building and allows easy detection of air leakage points in the building envelope. The air flow rate is measured at a number of pressure differentials from 20 to 50 P, and an air change rate is calculated in air changes per hour at a standard 50 P pressure differential. Unfortunately, there is no definite relation between this depressurised air change rate and the infiltration air change rate of the building under average climatic conditions. The latter depends on many properties of the building and its environment, such as the location of the leakage points, direction and strength of prevailing winds, and proximity of neighbouring structures. Statistical correlation indicates that the infiltration air change rate is usually about 5.5 less than the 50 P depressurisation rate.[8]

INDOOR AIR POLLUTION

In the past, concern over indoor air quality in nonindustrial buildings has been mostly a matter of comfort. Recently, with the trend to more tightly sealed buildings and the problems created by the use of new building materials, more attention is being paid to health and safety issues in residential buildings. Table 2.1[9] gives a list of sources of some key pollutants and their effects. Control of pollutants requires a combined effort from government, designer, builder, and occupier. The designer's role is mainly to specify benign materials and appliances, to control movement of moisture and radon gas with an effective air–vapour barrier, and to ensure adequate ventilation at around 0.5 air changes per hour. The designer must be particularly careful that materials introduced to improve energy efficiency, such as insulation, glazings, and heat exchanger components, do not themselves cause air quality deterioration.

Recent studies[10] have shown that most air quality problems are due to high pollutant sources rather than low air infiltration. New tight houses with 0.4 air changes per hour have about the same air quality as conventional new homes. The designer should particularly try to avoid products with high formaldehyde emission rates and ensure that all stoves and heating equipment are properly vented.

Radon gas, referred to in Table 2.1, is a radioactive daughter of uranium and occurs in low concentrations in most soils and masonry building materials. It is an

[8]Chia-Yu Shaw, A correlation between air infiltration and air tightness for houses in a developed residential area. *ASHRAE Trans.* **87**, 333–341 (1981).

[9]Table 2.1 is adapted from a paper by P. A. G. Russell, Indoor air pollutants — types, sources, and control. *Solar Energy Society of Canada Conference Proceedings 1984*, pp. 255–259.

[10]See *Solar Age* **11**(2), 33–35 (1986) and **11**(3), 33–37 (1986).

TABLE 2.1. Sources of Indoor Pollutants

Source	Typical pollutant	Effect	
		Discomfort	Health
Habits			
Smoking	1200+ components	X	X
Personal hygiene	Odours		
Lifestyle			
Cooking	Moisture, NOx		X
Cleaning materials	Hydrocarbons		X
Pesticides	Toxins		X
Hobbies	Hydrocarbons		X
Washing	Moisture		X
Inhabitants			
People	CO_2, moisture		
Pets	Bacteria, viruses	X	X
Equipment			
Appliances	Ozone		X
Furnishings	Formaldehyde	(X)	X
Building			
Heating and ventilation system	Products of combustion		X
	CO	life threatening	X
Off-gassing construction materials	Formaldehyde radon	(X)	X
External sources			
Soil	Soil, radon, moisture		X
Natural sources	Pollens, moisture	(X)	(X)
Agricultural and industrial emissions	Insect/herbicides		X
	SO_2		
Transport emissions	Lead, emissions		X

Note. Items in parentheses (X) indicate that the comfort or health effect is dependent on personal susceptibility

alpha emitter with a half-life of 4 days, and can cause lung cancer if breathed in. Most radon gas enters buildings from the soil through foundation walls and floors or via well water. The most effective way to keep it out is by eliminating paths for its entry. The number of joints in concrete pours should be as few as possible and they should be well caulked. The interior of block walls should be coated with an epoxy paint or a continuous film air–vapour barrier.

THERMAL INSULATION

The importance of insulation in the building envelope to restrict heat flow both in winter and summer is now generally recognised. The main purpose of a building is usually to protect its occupants from the natural elements, be it rain, snow, wind, heat, or cold. Most common building materials, such as brick, concrete, and wood, have relatively poor thermal insulating properties and need to be supplemented with special insulating materials. Most are light aerated materials, which obtain their thermal insulating properties from the myriad small air pockets rather than from the material itself. Another type of insulating material consists of several thin reflecting films, separated by thin air gaps.

Heat transfer can occur through three distinct physical methods: *conduction*, *convection*, and *radiation* (Figures 2.3–2.5). Conduction is the direct transfer of heat from one particle of a material to an adjacent one. Convection is the flow of heat

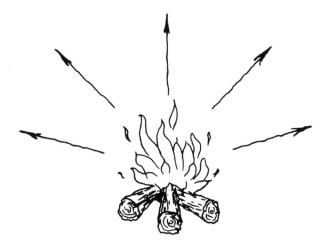

FIG. 2.3. Heat radiation

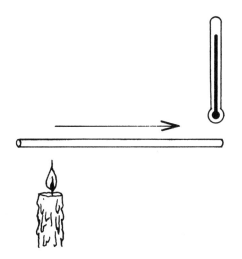

FIG. 2.4. Heat conduction

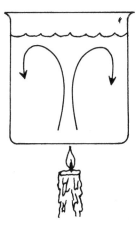

FIG. 2.5. Heat convection

by the actual movement of a liquid or gas. Because a warm fluid is lighter than a cool one, natural convection can occur when a fluid is heated from below, but natural stratification can also persist, with the warm layers at the top, and may need to be removed with a fan. (The most important exception to this is water below 4°C. The fact that water has a peak density at 4°C is of great practical importance, and creates opportunities for innovative natural methods for freeze protection.) Radiation is the transfer of heat directly from one surface to another without any effect by or on any intermediate medium, as when solar radiation impinges on the Earth. Radiative heat transfer is strongest from a hot surface, like the sun's, but it can also be significant at ordinary temperatures. Thus the "draught" that people may feel when sitting next to a cold window is usually not due to movement of cold air, but to heat being radiated from the warm body surface to the cold window surface.

Of the two main types of insulation, the aerated material effectively suppresses conduction and convection, whereas the thin-film material suppresses conduction and radiation but usually only partially suppresses convection.

Thermal insulation effectiveness is usually measured by a material's *thermal resistance*. As we discuss in chapter 7, thermal resistance is actually only a rather crude measure of insulation, but it is good enough for most purposes. English-speaking countries have traditionally used the British "R value," but this is now being replaced by the metric international system unit, the RSI, which is larger and equal to 5.68 R units. The thermal resistance of a material is directly proportional to its thickness, and, for a composite material, is simply the sum of the resistances of each component (Figure 2.6).

At the inside and outside surfaces, heat is transferred by radiation and convection with the surrounding air. As long as the surface temperatures are not too extreme, this surface heat transfer can itself be measured fairly well in terms of a surface thermal resistance, which is simply added to the material resistance. Because the outside of a building may be subject to varying winds, the outside surface thermal resistance is actually a varying quantity, and in simple practical calculations is given an average value considerably smaller than the inside surface resistance.

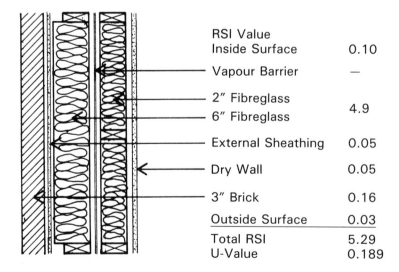

RSI Value	
Inside Surface	0.10
Vapour Barrier	—
2″ Fibreglass	
6″ Fibreglass	4.9
External Sheathing	0.05
Dry Wall	0.05
3″ Brick	0.16
Outside Surface	0.03
Total RSI	5.29
U-Value	0.189

FIG. 2.6. Composite wall—R and U values

The total rate of heat flow through the building structure is proportional to the cross-section area and the temperature difference between inside and outside and inversely proportional to the thermal resistance. Area divided by thermal resistance is called the *thermal transmittance,* or "*U* value." For any given space that is maintained at a constant temperature, an overall *U* value can be obtained by adding the individual values for walls, doors, windows, floors, and roofs.

Passive solar and energy-efficient buildings have much higher insulation values, and correspondingly lower *U* values than conventional buildings. The main practical implication of this is that walls need to be considerably thicker than usual to accommodate the extra insulation. Instead of 50×100 mm (2×4 in.) wood stud walls, 50×150 studs might be used, perhaps with further insulation on the inside of the studs as well as between the studs. Another method recently developed is the double frame wall, two separate 50×100 wall frames, with a 15 cm gap between them, so that a total of 35 cm of insulation can be installed. As interest in using higher insulation levels develops, other novel techniques of wall and roof construction will be developed. There does, however, seem to be a practical limitation, in that there is probably an upper limit of about 0.4 RSI per cm thickness of insulation material. If this is the case, then higher insulation levels will continue to require thicker walls.

Parts of the building envelope where the need for greater insulation is often overlooked are the foundation and basement walls and the doors. A standard 200 mm concrete block wall has a thermal resistance of only 0.3 RSI, and must be insulated up to at least 2 RSI, by adding extra insulation either on the inside or outside. It is sometimes stated that exterior insulation improves the thermal performance of the building by bringing the thermal mass of the concrete wall into the building. Our studies suggest that this effect is usually marginal, because the foundation thermal mass is normally too remote from the main living space. Generally, the choice of exterior or interior insulation should be made based mainly on convenience and cost.

Standard exterior wooden doors have a very low thermal resistance. If a door is protected by an exterior storm door, or a double air lock entry buffer zone, then its low resistance is not too serious; but if it is on its own, it should preferably be a modern insulated door. For any door that is opened much during a cold winter, the heat loss through air infiltration is much more serious than the normal conduction loss through the door. This is most effectively reduced by putting a double air lock entry buffer zone outside the door, with a second door opening to the ambient (Figure 2.7). One obvious implementation of this is the enclosed porch, which may be glazed or partially glazed depending on its orientation.

Passive solar buildings have larger than usual glazed areas in order to admit more solar energy into the building. Whereas a well-insulated wall might have a thermal resistance of 6 RSI or more, a single glazed window has only about 0.2 RSI. The thermal resistance increases roughly in proportion to the number of glazings, but solar energy transmitted decreases by about 15% for every glazing layer. In order to maintain reasonable *solar transmittance,* no more than two panes of glazing should normally be used on sun-facing windows, so these windows lose 15 times more heat than a similar area of wall. We shall see, in the computational chapters, that over a complete heating season a well designed solar window gains considerably more heat than it loses, but it can lose very large amounts of heat during sunless periods, such as at night or during overcast days.

Possible strategies for reducing heat loss from windows will be discussed later, but it should be mentioned that there is no reason in principle why much better windows cannot be designed, in which the thermal resistance is much increased while the solar

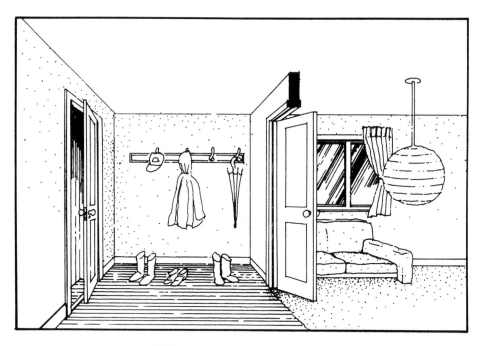

FIG. 2.7. Double door air lock entry

energy transmittance is maintained at high levels. Solar designers sometimes dream about transparent insulation, which behaves like normal insulation in strongly inhibiting the flow of heat, but also behaves like a single layer of glass in allowing most of the solar radiation striking it to pass through. Such a material does not violate physical principles and would be very useful to a passive solar designer, as we shall consider in more detail later. There has been considerable progress recently in the development of improved glazings, but we are still far short of a genuine transparent insulation.

FACTORY-BUILT HOUSES

High-quality factory building is well established in some countries, but rare in others. Energy efficiency is a top priority with some factory buildings. In Sweden, for example, RSI 5 walls and RSI 8 ceilings are common. It is fairly straightforward to provide insulation levels complete with long-life impervious vapour barrier in a prefabricated wall or ceiling. Super doors and windows can also be fitted as standard, together with an integral auxiliary heating system.

The ideal for a passive solar design would be standard prefabricated complete walls and roofs that could be assembled on site in various ways at the direction of the designer. Some limited progress has been made in this direction, but there are almost endless opportunities for further development.

CHAPTER 3

Heating and Cooling

SOLAR GAIN

Passive solar design attempts to increase the amount of useful solar energy that enters the building. The extra *solar gain* is achieved by large glazed areas, while the whole building design aims to ensure that the extra solar energy admitted can be put to useful purpose.

The obvious way to increase solar gain is to increase window area and to put most of the windows on the equator-facing side of the building, between southeast and southwest in the northern hemisphere, and between northeast and northwest in the southern hemisphere. East- and west-facing windows should normally be avoided, because although they do receive considerable amounts of solar radiation in spring and autumn, they are not very effective in midwinter and they receive maximum solar energy in midsummer, when it is not needed. It is possible to shade out the summer sun, so east and west windows may be useful in certain circumstances, but always as a second best choice to equator-facing windows.

Depending on latitude, equator-facing windows receive peak amounts of solar energy in early and late winter, and are very easy to shade in summer with simple overhangs. The sun-path diagrams at the end of the book show that the sun in north latitudes actually moves more slowly across the southern sky in the winter than it does in the summer. It is much lower in the sky in winter, and hence strikes a vertical window at a more normal angle, so that more solar radiation gets through the window than when the sun is high in the sky.

In addition to standard windows, several other types of glazed area may be used in passive solar buildings, as illustrated in Figures 3.1–3.4. The clerestory is a wide strip of windows, projecting up above a roof line, and admitting solar radiation to the sunless side of the building. The skylight is a hole in the roof, traditionally used mainly to admit light, but it can be redesigned to admit more winter heat as well.

Glazed areas may be either vertical or inclined. Maximum direct winter solar heat is admitted when the glazing is inclined to the horizontal at an angle 10°–20° greater than the latitude. However, there are several good reasons for choosing an angle of inclination nearer to the vertical than this. More reflected radiation from the ground

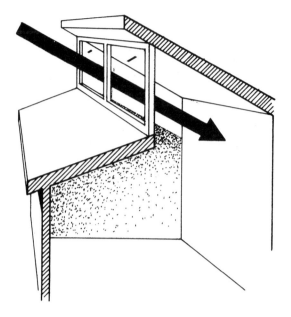

FIG. 3.1. Clerestory window

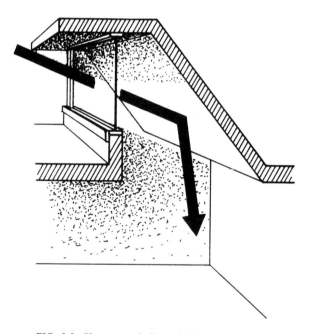

FIG. 3.2. Clerestory window with internal reflector

or roof surface penetrates a vertical area, particularly if there is snow cover for much of the winter. Second, as the inclination moves away from the vertical, summer solar gain increases, and it becomes more difficult to shade or insulate the glazing with curtains or blinds. Third, it becomes more difficult to seal the glazing against leaks, particularly from melting snow or ice. None of these reasons need necessarily rule

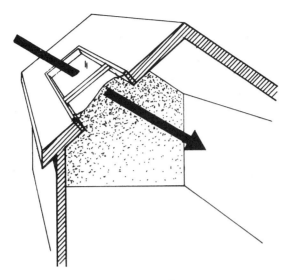

FIG. 3.3. Sloped skylight

FIG. 3.4. Horizontal skylight

out the use of inclined glazings, but the designer must be aware of their problems.

One particularly attractive use of an inclined glazing is in combination with an overhang reflector. This design is illustrated in chapter 5, where the general philosophy of using reflectors is discussed. In most cases, this particular reflector configuration is the most effective one.

INTERNAL HEAT GAINS

Internal heat gains can play a major role in heating an energy-efficient building. These gains come partly from people and animals and partly from heat-generating appliances. The total and time distribution of the gains depends very much on the type of building and the life-style of its occupants. Conventional heat-loss calculations have allowed for internal heat gains simply by using degree days below 18°C instead of the actual comfort temperature (usually 20–22°C). Typically, however, a superinsulated home might have a U value of 100 W/°C, and an average internal gain of 1000 W, with a corresponding average temperature increase of 10°C due to internal gains. The problem of actually calculating the effect of internal gains will be considered later, but it is appropriate to discuss their qualitative effects here.

During the midwinter period, internal gains help to reduce the auxiliary heat required to heat the building. In spring and autumn, they may supply all the heating requirements, thus reducing the length of the heating season. In summer, internal gains are unwanted and should be reduced as much as possible. A number of simple strategies are available to control internal gains, such as venting a clothes dryer to the inside in winter and to the outside in summer. A building designer can take certain steps to implement such strategies, but many of them constitute the life-style of the building occupants. Generally, a building designer should assume that only the minimum internal heat gains will be available to help meet the peak winter heat load.

Table 3.1 gives typical heat use per month by common domestic appliances. Except for the water heater, most of this heat eventually helps to heat the building. In normal use, it is usually estimated that about 10% of water heat goes into the building. Very simple life-style strategies, such as leaving hot baths and sinks for an hour before pulling the plug, can raise this fraction to about 50%. More complex waste water heat recovery procedures can recover most of the energy used to heat water.

The trend to more efficient appliances may soon render some of the data in Table 3.1 out of date. Some of the most efficient appliances can be found in the catalogues of photovoltaic and wind-energy supply companies. As the heat-gain contribution from more efficient appliances declines, there will be a corresponding need and opportunity for more passive solar gain.

THERMAL MASS (HEAT CAPACITY)

Thermal mass is the ability of a material to store heat. As the material absorbs heat, its temperature rises, and the heat it can absorb for a 1°C temperature rise is the real thermal mass of the material. Some materials can absorb heat without temperature rise, as the heat is used either to change the phase of the material from solid

TABLE 3.1. Appliances — Monthly Consumption

Appliance	Average kW/hr use/month
Furnace fan — continuous operation	182
Frost-free refrigerator	140
Upright freezer (frost-free)	107
Water heater	100/person
Chest freezer (16 cu. ft)	84
Furnace fan	66
Range	65
Clothes dryer	40/person
Manual defrost refrigerator	56
Dishwasher	40
Colour television	30
Electric kettle	20
Toaster oven	20
Humidifier (power with fan)	15

to liquid or liquid to gas, or to cause a chemical change. Phase change or chemical thermal mass have considerable potential for use in passive solar design, but have not yet been used much in practice.

Thermal mass is ignored in conventional heat loss analysis, because it is not important if all temperatures are held constant. Thermal mass obviously becomes important in passive solar design when temperatures are allowed to vary in order to store solar heat for later use. Even in conventional building design, however, thermal mass does have some effects. As ambient temperature changes, the temperature of the building structure changes with some time delay due to its thermal mass, and the building interior does not "see" the full effect of a short dip in ambient temperature, such as might occur overnight.

Every building has some thermal mass that can store a certain amount of solar heat. If considerable amounts of solar heat are to be stored, however, it is desirable to add to the thermal mass of the building. Some of the more common thermal mass components are shown in Figure 3.5, along with typical values. The most common materials to provide extra thermal mass are water, masonry, concrete, and earth. Water has a thermal mass of 1.2 kWhr/m^3/°C, whereas each of the others has a thermal mass about one third that of water. Water is therefore the most effective material, but it does require a special container and is not a normal building material. One simple way of adding extra thermal mass is to use an extra thickness of drywall on the inside of the exterior walls and interior partitions.

Traditional native architecture in many parts of the world has used heavy thick walls made of stone, adobe, or earth, combined with well-insulated roofs, often made of thatched straw. This is very effective in warm arid climates that have reasonably cool summer nights and not too severe winters. The high thermal mass of the walls effectively averages out the heat of the day and the cool of night inside the building. In summer, most solar radiation strikes the insulated roof and does not significantly heat the building interior. In winter the sun is lower in the sky, warms up the thick walls, and thus indirectly heats the building interior.

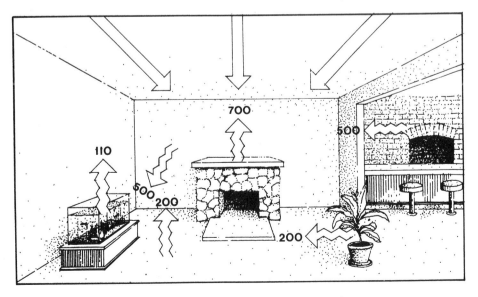

FIG. 3.5. Extra thermal mass in building interior

TABLE 3.2. Building Materials — Thermal Mass

	Specific heat kJ/kg × °C*	Thermal capacity kJ/m³ × °C
Brick	0.84	1655.2
Concrete	0.65	1499.5
Rock	0.43	1169.7
Steel	0.50	3916.9
Water	4.19	4188.3
Wood (oak)	2.39	1799.4

*The Joule (J) is a wattsecond, the energy provided by 1 W in 1 sec. Generally it is more convenient to use the hour as a time unit. To convert from kJ to Whr, divide by 3.6.

This traditional heavy wall architecture is not appropriate for places with cold winters, because the walls are poor thermal insulators. The Trombe wall described in chapters 4 and 6 can be considered as an attempt to extend heavy-wall architecture to cooler climates by putting a layer of glazing on the outside of the sun-facing wall. This retains most of the winter solar energy collection of the wall and markedly reduces the heat loss from the wall surface. However, as we shall see, even the Trombe wall type of heavy-wall architecture is not very effective in severe winter climates.

When a special thermal mass wall or floor is added to a building, it is often stated that direct sunlight must strike the thermal mass. Several authors[11] say that four times as much thermal mass is required if it is not in direct sunlight, and that this requirement is a possible problem in passive solar retrofits to an existing building.

However, thermal mass inside a building actually serves two distinct purposes. It prevents short-term overheating while the sun is shining, and it provides longer-term storage to heat the building overnight and possibly through succeeding cloudy days. Our studies indicate that direct sunlight helps to reduce short-term overheating by a few degrees Celsius, but it has no significant effect on long-term storage.

More important than direct sunlight on the thermal mass is the thermal accessibility of the thermal mass. A thin masonry wall of large surface area is much more effective in reducing overheating than a thick wall with the same total volume. These effects are quantified in a later chapter.

Table 3.2 gives the thermal masses of common building materials.

SOLAR HOT WATER

Hot water can be supplied either by conventional means or from active or passive solar collection. In most buildings, the need for hot water is fairly steady through the year, so summer sunshine can be utilised. In climates where no winter freeze protection is needed, an improved breadbox-type passive collector (Figure 3.6), a thermosiphon passive collector, or a simple cheap active collector is worth serious consideration. In more severe climates, winter freeze protection adds to the cost and creates further possibilities for unreliability. In locations with severe winters but sunny summers, it may be worthwhile to install a summer-only solar water heater. In some parts of North America, such a heater can provide more than 80% of the

---

[11]Authors who stress the importance of direct sunlight striking thermal mass include Mazria, *The Passive Solar Energy Book*; Argue, *The Well-Tempered House*; Anderson and Riordan, *The Solar Home Book*.

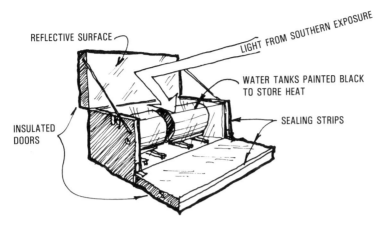

FIG. 3.6. Breadbox type passive solar water heater

solar hot water that would be available from an annual freeze-protected collector at considerably greater cost.

In Saunders' sandwich design, described in chapter 4, solar preheating of domestic hot water is an integral part of the solar space heating in the attic.

PASSIVE COOLING

The most fundamental principle in passive cooling is to shade the building, especially the windows, from the summer sun. This principle applies everywhere summer heat is a potential problem. Reflective foil in the attic can significantly reduce the transfer of summer heat into the building and also helps to cut radiative heat losses in winter.

A fixed overhang over an equator-facing window can be designed so that it shades the window completely in midsummer and leaves it totally unshaded in midwinter. The design angles depend of course on latitude, but there must always be a vertical separation between the bottom of the overhang and the top of the window. The common overhang, flush with the top of the window, will always shade the window, even in midwinter, and should be avoided (Figure 3.7).

A variable seasonally adjusted overhang is much more versatile than a fixed one. One simple, effective shading strategy is a small fixed overhang that admits sunshine through 3 or 4 winter months with a canvas curtain hooked to the overhang in midsummer.

An effective method of restricting solar gain in a large commercial or industrial building is to spray water on the roof at a rate of about 2 kg per square meter per hour, possibly using waste-process water. This method of evaporative cooling is most effective in warm, humid climates where air-conditioning loads are often very large.

In regions where summer nights are generally cool, a well-insulated building with adequate thermal mass will tend to remain at the average daily temperature, which may well be comfortable enough. Further cooling can be obtained by opening windows or ventilators to the cool night air and also perhaps using fans.

Summer sunshine itself can be used to induce air movement through a building. For example, in the Saunders' sandwich design, described in chapter 4, the summer opening of a vent in the attic not only helps to cool the attic, but permits solar energy

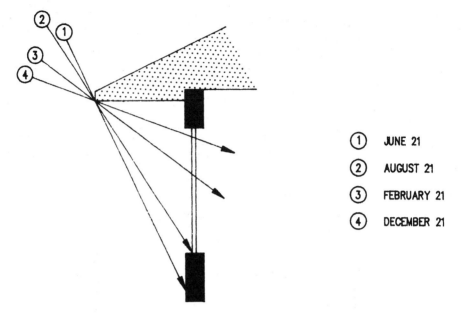

FIG. 3.7a. Correct overhang arrangement

① JUNE 21
② AUGUST 21
③ FEBRUARY 21
④ DECEMBER 21

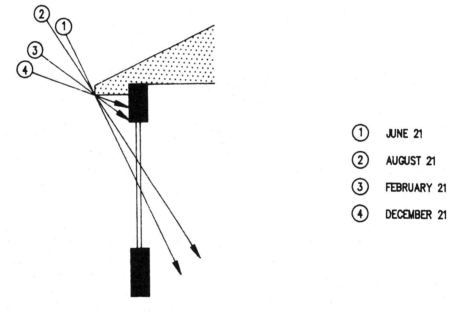

FIG. 3.7b. Incorrect overhang arrangement

① JUNE 21
② AUGUST 21
③ FEBRUARY 21
④ DECEMBER 21

reaching the sun space to establish air circulation through the entire building. As discussed in chapter 1, air movement can increase comfort even if it does not lower temperatures at all.

The location of vents and partitions can help to improve natural ventilation. If possible, the intake vent should be placed on the windward side of the building and the outlet vent on the leeward side. The outlet vent should be somewhat larger than the intake. Interior partitions should be arranged so that air movement between intake and outlet vents will occur throughout the whole interior space of the building.

The most difficult challenge for passive cooling is in a region where both summer temperatures and humidities may remain high for long periods. Cooling by air movement requires greater air flows and will probably need a fan. Earth tempering may often be useful. About 2 m down, the undisturbed earth remains at about the average annual temperature all year. If this average temperature is below 20°C, the earth may be used to cool and dehumidify a building in summer. If the building is built partly underground (e.g., a basement), then cool air may be drawn from the underground area through the building. Otherwise, air may be drawn through earth tubes buried underground. Research[12] has shown that an earth tube should be about 50 cm in diameter, buried about 2 m deep, and should be about 50 m long. It should slope down away from the building, with a drainage hole at its lowest point to permit seepage of condensed moisture from the cooled air.

In both the partly underground use and the earth tubes, the earth-cooled air may be drawn through the building either by naturally induced convection or by fans. Because the thermal conductivity of earth is rather low, the cooling capacity of any earth-cooled system is limited by the surface area in contact with the earth. If the earth-cooling system does not function at night, there will be time for more "coolth" to flow from deeper earth to the earth tube or underground part of the building.

Earth cooling is most effective in early and midsummer, when the earth around a building is still cool from the effects of winter. In many locations, nights become significantly cooler in late summer, so earth cooling can then be supplemented or replaced by night ventilation. Some of the traditional "designing with climate" concepts discussed in chapter 1 are particularly relevant to passive cooling.

AUXILIARY HEATING AND COOLING

Auxiliary heating and cooling of a passive solar building differs from conventional practice in several ways. The size of the auxiliary system required should be much smaller than usual, probably between 20 and 50 W of heating per square meter of floor space in most climates, and usually little or no cooling load at all. The use of individual room heaters and air conditioners is often advisable, because most passive solar designs accept or even encourage different temperatures in different zones of the building. Many designers have reported that the substantial capital savings on a smaller heating system can pay for extra passive solar design features.

The choice of auxiliary heating fuel depends partly on relative fuel costs in the particular location, but if electricity is at all competitive, there is much to be said for its use. Electricity is easily controlled in several different zones and is easily provided in the relatively small units required. Solar designers who have an ethical objection to the possible environmental damage done by the electricity supply industry should recognise that the auxiliary heating loads are small in a well-designed passive solar building, and may well be small compared with the other electrical loads in the building.

Fuel oil, kerosene, natural gas, propane, and wood can all be satisfactory auxiliary fuels in certain circumstances, but there may be difficulty in obtaining sufficiently

[12]A rather discouraging description of earth tubes is in Marguerite Smolen, The truth about cool tubes. *New Shelter* **5**(6), 57–59 (1984). For calculations on earth-tube effectiveness, see A. L. T. Serva da Motta and A. N. Young, A revised method for predicting the effectiveness of buried pipe cooling systems in buildings. *Intersol 85 Proceedings* **2**, 759–763 (1986).

small appliances. An oversized furnace will cycle on and off very frequently, and this may substantially reduce the overall combustion efficiency and generate undesirable pollution. Integrated gas units, which became available in the mid-1980s, provide both space and water heating and are an attractive option. There are also interesting developments in units that use heat wasted in one process to power another one, as, for example, exhaust refrigeration heat to preheat domestic hot water. Wood stoves need to be very carefully chosen, installed, and maintained to ensure adequate fire hazard and pollution control.

In a well-designed passive solar building, the auxiliary heat load is so low that it is difficult to justify the extra capital cost of some of the more recent energy-efficient heating appliances, such as condensing gas furnaces or ground-source heat pumps. Even the cooling capability of a heat pump will rarely, if ever, be needed in most climates.

Until commercial active solar cooling units are widely available, electricity will probably be the main force for any auxiliary cooling needed. The solar enthusiast might consider generating electricity from photovoltaic cells, especially for a summer application such as cooling and air conditioning. In most locations these are not currently economic, but they may be in the 1990s. It is a wise precaution to leave roof space for possible retrofit of photovoltaic panels if and when they become economical.

CHAPTER 4

Passive Solar Building Types

Passive solar building designs can be classified according to the main mechanisms for collecting and storing solar heat. The main types are discussed here, but any actual building may be intermediate between types or may incorporate attributes of several different types. In no circumstances should the building designer allow this type classification to restrict his or her creativity.

Various research groups, such as the Solar Energy Research Institute and the Berkeley Building Energy Data Group in the United States,[13] have collected monitoring data that show that all solar building types perform well when properly designed and constructed. Generally, the various passive designs have outperformed designs using active solar collectors.

Energy monitoring, however, is only part of the picture, and it is dangerous to believe all the merits of any design can be summarized in a few numbers. A good design, particularly a solar design, involves many factors that are difficult or impossible to quantify.

SUPERINSULATED PASSIVE SOLAR BUILDINGS

A superinsulated building, shown in Figure 4.1, has insulation levels in the walls and ceilings of 8 RSI or more. Special attention is paid to sealing and vapour-barrier installation to reduce uncontrolled air infiltration to 0.2 air changes per hour or less. This usually requires the installation of mechanical ventilation or an air-to-air heat exchanger, which provides adequate controlled ventilation by using exiting warm stale air to heat the entering cold fresh air. Glazed areas are conventional windows whose area does not exceed 7% of building floor area, but they are oriented with passive solar gain in mind. Usually, no extra thermal mass is added. A typical home of 120 m^2 floor area in a location with 5,000 heating degree days Celsius, might have a total annual heating load of 35 GJ (about 10,000 kWhr). About 15 GJ would be generated from appliances, 5 GJ from people, 7 GJ from passive solar gain, which

[13]Results from the U.S. passive monitoring program are given in Michael Holtz, Ronald Frey, Robert Bishop, and Joel Swisher, The future of passive solar design. *Solar Age* **10**(10), 49–56 (1985).

FIG. 4.1. Superinsulated solar-tempered house. This type of house looks quite conventional, except for the preponderance of windows on the sun-facing side and the extra-thick walls.

leaves 8 GJ to be provided by an auxiliary heating system. Because in many locations the winter solar radiation falling on the building would be around 250 GJ, the superinsulated home utilises only a small fraction of the potential solar gain available.

DIRECT GAIN PASSIVE SOLAR BUILDINGS

A direct gain building has larger than usual glazed areas, mostly sun facing, so that the incident solar radiation "directly" heats the building (Figure 4.2). Insulation and sealing levels are higher than normal, but not as high as in the superinsulated design. Extra thermal mass is added to store the enhanced solar gain, and the building may or may not be divided into temperature zones. Some of the larger glazed areas may be provided with movable night insulation.

FIG. 4.2. Direct gain passive solar house

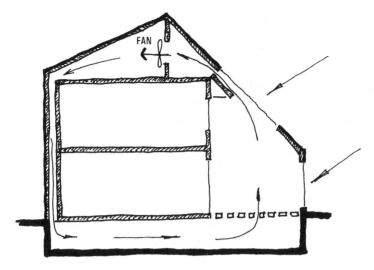

FIG. 4.3. Double envelope passive solar house

This design can work very well, but is subject to various possible problems. There can be serious overheating in all seasons if the mass and glass are not balanced correctly. Conversely the design concept can be thwarted if the building occupants draw blinds or curtains to keep out what they consider to be unwanted sunshine. Fading of fabrics exposed to bright sunshine can be a problem that can be resolved through choice of special fabrics and dyes or through use of glazings that cut down on ultraviolet transmission.

Double Envelope Building

This is a direct gain building with a hollow envelope all the way around the south and north walls, floor, and ceiling (Figure 4.3). The original designers claimed that air warmed by the sun circulated around the space in the envelope, thus heating the building mainly by low temperature radiation from the walls. The actual mechanism for the performance of these buildings is still controversial,[14] but most people who have studied it now believe that there is no significant air circulation through the envelope, and that the design is really a combination of direct gain and superinsulation. The unconventional design and construction give the architect full scope for creative design, which some people may find very attractive. The hollow envelope is a potential fire hazard and a possible nesting place for insects and small animals.

The Sun Space

The sun space goes under various names, such as a solarium, atrium, conservatory, or greenhouse. It is usually a large space with a large glazed area facing the sun, and is usually connected or integrated with the main living areas in the building (Figure 4.4). Some or all of the glazing is commonly inclined to the vertical. As its var-

---

[14]See William A. Shurcliff, *Superinsulated Houses and Double-Envelope Houses*. Brick House, Andover, MA, 1981. An article by John Hughes, The double envelope faces a death blow. *Solar Age* **10**(4), 20–21 (1985) reports better performance when the convective loop is blocked off!

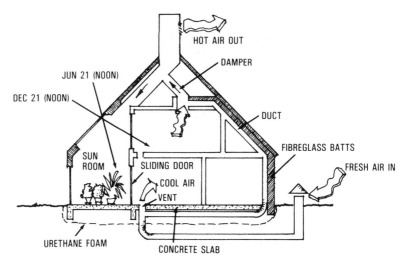

FIG. 4.4. Attached sun space

ious names imply, the space may be used for a variety of purposes, but it normally has the distinctive feature that temperatures are allowed to vary much more than in a normal living space. The sun space would not normally be occupied by people either during a sunny spell or during a cold night. The space may have some extra thermal mass to maintain reasonable night temperatures, or it may be provided with fans to transfer warm air into the main living spaces when required. If plants are to be grown in the sun space, some auxiliary heating may be provided to maintain temperatures above a certain minimum. The large glazed areas are not usually provided with night insulation.

The Underground Passive Solar Building

Like the double envelope building, the underground building has its enthusiasts and its detractors. The usual concept is a building surrounded top, bottom, and side by earth, except for the sun-facing side, which is heavily glazed (Figure 4.5). The enthusiasts emphasize that the large thermal mass of the earth surrounding the building has a moderating effect on temperatures both in winter and summer. The detractors say that if you dig a hole in the ground, it usually fills with water; and who wants

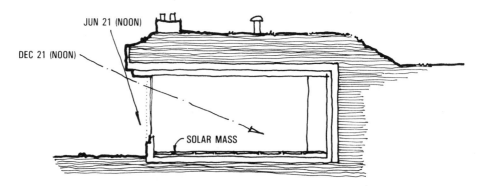

FIG. 4.5. Underground passive solar home

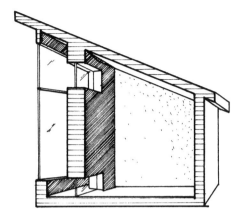

FIG. 4.6. Indirect gain — Trombe wall

to live in a pond! Also, the often-repeated statement that the ground a few meters down maintains a uniform temperature is somewhat misleading, because it is really true only for undisturbed ground, without any building in it and without any underground water flows. The underground building can be satisfactory if well designed on a well-chosen site, but it also offers the potential for big mistakes.

INDIRECT GAIN — TROMBE WALL

The Trombe (or mass) wall, named after Felix Trombe's pioneering efforts in southern France,[15] is a thick masonry wall on the sun-facing side of the building, and glazed on the outside (Fig. 4.6).

A detailed technical description of the Trombe wall is reserved for a later chapter, but the basic principle is that solar heat slowly permeates through the wall and into the building. Depending on wall thickness, the heat flow into the building is almost uniform (thick wall) or peaks in the early evening after a sunny day (thin wall). The mass wall may be of water rather than masonry and may have vents top and bottom to increase heat flow into the building through air circulation.

Except in mild climates, the Trombe wall does not utilise solar energy very efficiently, because the hot outer wall surface radiates much of the heat collected back out through the glazing. Efficiency is improved considerably by use of movable night insulation. In spite of its low efficiency, the Trombe wall is a useful alternative or adjunct to a direct gain system, particularly for people who find intense sunshine unpleasant in a living area.

INDIRECT GAIN — ROOF PONDS

The original roof pond concept (Figure 4.7 left), developed by Harold Hay in Arizona,[16] is a pond of water on the flat roof of a building. In the heating mode in winter, the pond absorbs solar energy during the day and then radiates it down into the building. It is covered with movable insulation at night. In the summer, the pond

---

[15]A fairly detailed account of the early work of Felix Trombe and Jacques Michel at Odeillo, France is given in Bruce Anderson, *The Solar Home Book*. Cheshire Books, Harrisville, NH, 1976.

[16]Bruce Anderson's *Solar Home Book* is also a good source for a description of Harold Hay's early work on the roof pond.

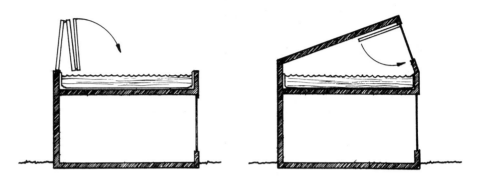

FIG. 4.7. (Left) Original roof pond; (right) cold climate roof pond

is screened during the day and uncovered at night so that heat can be radiated out to the sky.

A cold-climate version of the roof pond essentially has the pond inside an attic with the sun-facing roof of the attic glazed and the inside of the other roof surface reflecting. The glazing may have a movable insulating shutter as illustrated in Figure 4.7, right.

In spite of Hay's claims that roofs can readily be designed to support the roof pond load, there is probably a psychological barrier to the roof pond. No matter what engineering reassurances may be forthcoming, many people feel uncomfortable with a large mass of water over their heads.

SAUNDERS' SOLAR SANDWICH

This design[17] uses a sun space from which solar heat is convected into an attic space containing drums of water. This water is the high temperature store (30–40°C), well insulated from the outside and partially insulated from the building interior. As necessary, heat is blown with a fan from the attic into the low-temperature rock store under the floor, in order to maintain the rocks around 20°C. The rocks play only a minor role in heating the building, but they can also be used for cooling.

Later versions[18] of the Saunders' design use drums of water for the underfloor low-temperature storage, as well as for the attic thermal storage. The authors' experience with an experimental version of this design[19] showed that it can be difficult to transfer sufficient solar heat into the attic thermal storage, and we were never able to maintain attic temperatures much above 20°C. We were successful, however, in keeping the building cool in the summer by natural air circulation, powered by solar energy collected in the sun space. This suggests that the concept needs further development before it can be considered a routine design.

As we discuss in chapter 10, the solar sandwich and other related designs have the potential to store solar heat for several days, and thus to provide close to complete solar heating. As shown in Figure 4.8, substantial solar preheating of domestic hot water may be achieved by putting the tank in the attic.

[17]William A. Shurcliff, Saunders' 100%-solar, low cost design, in *Super Solar Homes*. Brick House, Andover, MA, 1983.
[18]For recent Saunders' designs see David Kauffman, 100% solar in Maine. *Solar Age* **11**(3), 24–27 (1986).
[19]R. Bennet, C. Carter, and J. de Villiers, Design, construction, simulation, and economics of a super-solar building. *Intersol 85 Proceedings*, **1**, 146–150 (1986).

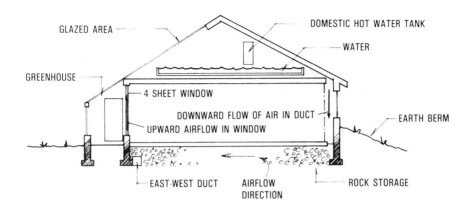

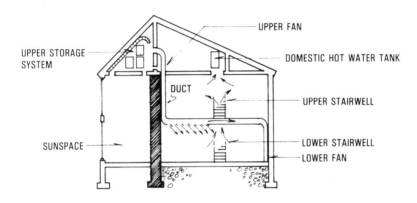

FIG. 4.8. Two versions of Saunders' solar sandwich: (top) with glazed attic; (bottom) with insulated attic

COMMERCIAL BUILDING PASSIVE DESIGN

Recent standard commercial buildings typically have a completely artificially controlled environment. There does seem to be a trend back to more natural designs incorporating some passive solar features. Direct gain and mass wall systems are generally not very suitable for commercial designs, but the atrium, in its many varied forms, holds great promise. The atrium might be a large glazed space on the south face of the building or a roof-glazed space over an interior void separating two or more parts of the building, and it clearly lends itself to imaginative design. In most climates, the atrium is a net energy loser if its interior temperature is controlled within normal interior building limits. It can be a net energy saver, however, if it is considered as a tempered space with fairly large temperature variations allowed. A tempered atrium has similarities to the sun space in the Saunders' solar sandwich design, and we might expect that modifications of the Saunders' design would be particularly appropriate for commercial buildings.

Natural daylighting is a particular concern in large commercial buildings, especially in summer, when the elimination of artificial lighting can drastically reduce cooling loads.

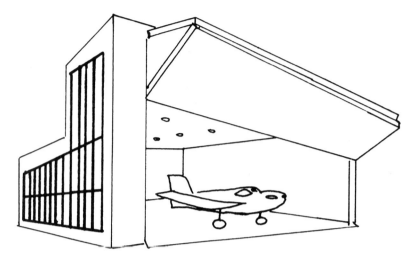

FIG. 4.9. Air Ketchum solar hangar

The design requirement for small commercial buildings is generally similar to that of houses, except that the buildings are usually unoccupied during the night and weekends. Commercial designers should determine initially whether a large single building is really needed, or whether a number of smaller house-like buildings might be more appropriate and more attractive.

The Air Ketchum solar hangar,[20] illustrated in Figure 4.9, has a floor area of 600 m^2, with high insulation levels, RSI 10 in walls and ceiling, and is heated by the solar gain through 100 m^2 of south-facing glass. The only supplementary energy is about 40 GJ per year for lights and fans. Inside temperatures vary between 13 and 27°C, while ambient temperatures vary from −37 to 32°C. This building is a vivid demonstration of the greater potential of passive solar gain when interior temperatures are allowed to vary more than would be acceptable for continuous human occupation.

OTHER INNOVATIVE DESIGNS

The essential feature of both the roof pond and the solar sandwich is that the long-term high temperature thermal storage is partially insulated from the living space; this enables solar heat to be stored for several days without overheating the living space. Various other means for achieving this have been suggested, such as composite floors, mechanically coupled rock beds, and use of phase-change materials. We will not attempt to catalogue all the ideas, but merely comment that there is tremendous scope for human ingenuity in this area, particularly in the design of passive solar commercial buildings. Most of the quantitative material in Part 2 of this book is offered as a means to encourage innovative ideas, and allow them to be assessed quantitatively.

---

[20]The Air Ketchum solar hangar. *Sunworld* 9(1), 20–21 (1985).

CHAPTER 5

Windows and Reflectors

WINDOWS FOR SOLAR HEATING AND DAYLIGHTING

Window size and orientation have been discussed in chapter 2. Windows allow light and solar heat to enter a building, but they also allow internal heat to escape rather readily to the outside. In some cases, windows are also a main method of providing ventilation for the building. In fact, until the 18th century, most windows were just small openings in the wall to permit daylight and fresh air to enter. They were boarded up at night and during bad weather. As the technology for making glass improved, glass windows gradually became cheaper and larger; now they are almost universally used. Various plastic alternatives to glass have been developed in recent years, but none as yet have successfully challenged glass for its overall qualities of light transmission and durability. Some plastic glazings have higher transmissivity than glass, but poor durability. They may be used most effectively as inner layers in multilayer glazings.

In a passive solar building, the sun-facing window is the solar collector. For reasons discussed earlier, the sun-facing windows should normally face within 30° of due south (in the northern hemisphere). Some designers favour an orientation slightly angled to the east in order to collect useful solar energy early in the day, but this effect is marginal. East- or west-facing windows are generally undesirable because they collect little solar energy in midwinter and need to be shaded from the intense summer sunshine. They do, however, collect considerable amounts of solar energy in early and late winter, spring, and autumn, and may be useful in certain circumstances.

Windows facing away from the sun should be eliminated or kept small, because they are net heat losers. Narrow strip windows can be useful for providing daylight in parts of the building remote from the sun-facing windows. Although such windows are net heat losers in winter, they may still be worthwhile, insofar as they avoid the need for heat-generating artificial light in summer. Because most useful light in a room comes from above, daylighting windows should normally be set high in the wall. Venetian blinds can also be used to reflect incoming light up onto the ceiling. In some cases, daylighting windows might be continuously shuttered during the winter. Windows are, of course, used in buildings to reveal a pleasant outside view as well as to admit heat and light. For this purpose small windows are often adequate, either narrow horizontal strips or narrow vertical strips.

There is much to be said for the conventional window mounted in a vertical plane, for the reasons outlined in the "Solar Gain" section in chapter 3. However, another conventional practice of having many windows that can be opened is more questionable. It is difficult to seal adequately such windows against air leaks, and ventilation can be provided more satisfactorily through special ventilation louvres.

Maximum direct solar radiation over a heating season is received through a window mounted in a plane inclined to the horizontal at 10° to 20° more than the latitude. Diffuse radiation, however, is greatest for a horizontal window, whereas ground- or roof-reflected radiation is greatest for a vertical window. Summer solar gain increases as the inclination angle departs from the vertical and increases the need for summer shading. The overall result of these competing effects is that window inclination is usually kept close to the vertical. The exact angle is not critical.

Sun-collecting windows are also major losers of heat when the sun is not shining. Heat transfer between the panes of a standard multipane window is roughly equally divided between convection and radiation. Generally a window will collect two to three times as much solar energy as it loses in heat over a heating season, but anything that can be done to reduce the heat losses or increase the solar gain will markedly improve the overall energy performance of the building. Useful strategies include increasing the number of glazings, surface films, convection suppression, movable insulation, and external reflectors. Each will be considered in turn.

Every extra pane of glazing reduces both convective and radiative heat loss; in fact, the overall thermal resistance of a standard window is approximately 0.18 RSI for each pane. However, surface reflection at each air-glazing interface and absorption within the glazing material reduces the amount of solar radiation transmitted through the glazing (Figure 5.1). For normal glass, about 14% of transmission is lost for every pane of glazing. Low iron glass loses only 9% for each pane, whereas for some plastic glazing materials, the loss may be as low as 5% per pane.

In most climates, it is desirable to add a second pane of glazing to a solar window, but further panes usually reduce the solar gain more than they save in heat loss. For nonsolar windows, two or more panes may be used, depending on the climate and if any other means are used to reduce loss.

In order to reduce significantly the heat loss through a window, it is necessary to reduce both convective and radiative heat losses. Convective loss can be reduced by lowering the gas pressure and/or inserting a plastic heat trap between glazings. The heat trap can take the form of a honeycomb or simple horizontal layers of plastic (Figure 5.2). Detailed studies[21] have shown that convection is almost completely suppressed if the aspect ratio d/h is sufficiently large, around 10 or greater. Ideally, the plastic used should be transparent to visible light, but should also absorb heat radiation. In this case, the heat trap also suppresses most of the radiative loss through the window, as well as the convective loss. The heat trap window is necessarily thick overall, usually 15 cm or more, and it requires the use and installation of rather large amounts of plastic sheet. Various manufacturers have attempted to market a heat trap window, but in the mid-1980s none are clearly economically competitive.

Radiative loss may be reduced by use of thin surface films or coatings on the

---

[21]K. G. T. Hollands and K. Tynkaran, Proposal for a compound honeycomb collector. *Solar Energy* 34, 309–316 (1985).

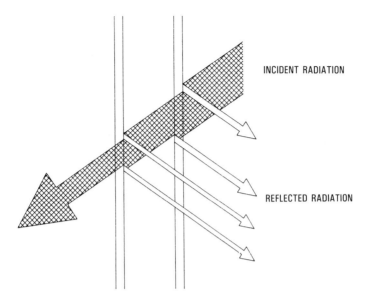

FIG. 5.1. Multipane reflection and absorption

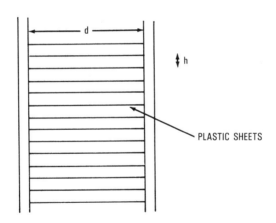

FIG. 5.2. Heat trap glazing

glazed panes. For maximising useful solar gain, films are chosen that will transmit a high proportion of the solar radiation but reflect most of the low temperature thermal radiation. Films are more commonly used today to reduce solar gain in summer. These solar-control films can screen out as much as three quarters of incident solar radiation, and should not be used on any windows designed to collect solar energy in winter.

SUPERGLAZINGS

Heat mirror (low-*e*) films or coatings currently under development are designed to transmit most solar radiation but reflect heat radiation. Unlike normal glass, which absorbs heat radiation, glass or plastic treated with a heat mirror film reflects heat radiation back into the building. The glass remains very cold in winter and is a potential source of condensation, especially if the film is on an inside surface. Windows have been manufactured with a plastic heat mirror film between two panes of glass, with an RSI of about 0.5. This design avoids the condensation problem and also protects the sensitive heat mirror film from degradation.

A recent manufacturing process, called pyrolitic or hard-coat, fuses the low-*e* coating onto the glass.[22] This produces a much more durable product, but with slightly inferior energy performance. Currently, the best low-*e* double pane glass has about the same transmittance for solar radiation (0.75) and the same insulating value (RSI 0.5) as standard triple glazing, so it has few advantages for solar windows in buildings. Current research and development is attempting to produce a superglazing with the solar transmittance of double glazing (0.82) but with double the insulating value of triple glazing (RSI 1.0); it seems quite likely that this will be achieved within a few years.

In principle, it should be possible to reduce both convective and radiative losses through windows to very low levels, while maintaining solar transmission. As we discuss in chapter 10, this could be a big boost for passive solar design. An interesting possibility is that even a polar-facing window, receiving only diffuse and reflected sunlight, could yield a net energy gain, with solar gains exceeding heat losses.

MOVABLE INSULATION

Another approach to reducing heat loss through windows is the use of movable insulation, which is put in place at night and possibly during overcast days, and can also be used to screen out unwanted solar gain in summer. Movable insulation can take many different forms such as curtains, blinds, internal or external shutters, or plastic beads blown between the panes (Figure 5.3). No single method has become dominant in the mid-1980s, and none has emerged that is clearly economic in all circumstances. Standard insulating materials are very bulky, and their storage when not in use often presents an aesthetic if not a space problem. The multiple reflecting film blind is an interesting alternative because it compresses to reasonable size for storage. In order to be effective, interior movable insulation must be well sealed with the window frame to prevent air circulation between the building interior and the window. Even standard heavy curtains can be useful insulators as long as they are sealed at the top and sides. The importance of movable insulation will be studied in more detail in chapter 9.

SAUNDERS' SOLAR STAIRCASE

The staircase[23] is an attic solar window consisting of multiple layers of transparent plastic and air spaces behind a glass surface and a set of reflective louvres (Figure 5.4a). In the winter, midday sunlight enters the attic by direct transmission. Some of the radiation reflected back by the plastic layer surfaces hits a reflective louvre and is reflected back down into the attic (Figure 5.4b), so that reflection losses are partially suppressed.

When the sun is low in the sky, the louvres reflect the rays indirectly into the attic

---

[22]Day Chahroudie, The future of high-performance glazings. *Solar Age* **11**(2), 21–26 (1986). This is an upbeat description written by an enthusiastic pioneer in developing new glazings.
[23]The Saunders staircase is described in Shurcliff's book (Note 17).

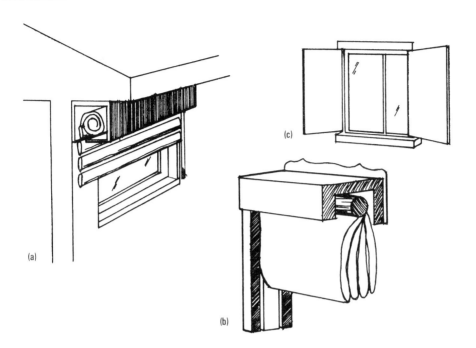

FIG. 5.3. Types of movable insulation: (a) External shutter; (b) internal shutter; (c) multilayer blind

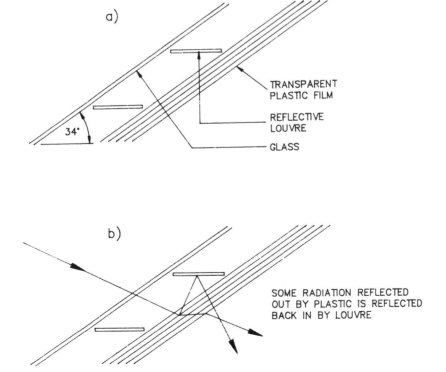

FIG. 5.4. (a) Solar staircase detail; (b) winter – direct transmission

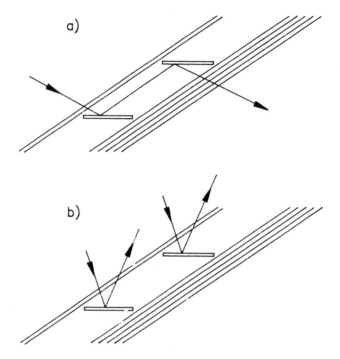

FIG. 5.5. (a) Winter—indirect transmission; (b) summer—reflection to sky

space (Figure 5.5a). In the summer, when the sun is much higher in the sky, the louvres reflect much of the unwanted direct radiation back to the sky (Figure 5.5b).

In his patented implementation of the solar staircase, Saunders has used an inclination angle of 34° with the horizontal. With this low angle, his computer calculations predict that the suppression of internal reflection losses increases the overall transmission of solar radiation through a six-pane window (one glass and five plastic sheets) from its normal 50% to around 70%. However, reflection loss suppression requires the inclination angle to be less than 40°, so the solar staircase has rather limited applications.

EXTERNAL REFLECTORS

There is a large literature[24] on the use of reflectors to enhance solar gain through a window, but very little actual practice. Reflectors are, of course, an essential part of active tracking concentrating solar collectors. When used with fixed windows, most fixed reflector configurations may boost solar gain at some times, but shade it out at other times, so that they cause little improvement overall. There are two main reflector configurations that can be effective. On windows oriented partly towards the east or west, external vertical reflectors roughly normal to the window along its polar edge boost solar gain in midwinter, and reduce it in summer (Figure 5.6). Imaginative architectural design is required to integrate this type of reflector with the building, and prevent it from becoming an ugly obtrusion.

---

[24]See, for example, W. T. Welford and R. Winston, *The Optics of Nonimaging Concentrators*. Academic, New York, 1978.

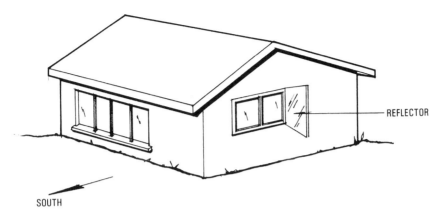

SOUTH

FIG. 5.6. Vertical reflector on east or south–east window

The second effective reflector/window configuration is an inclined reflector above a sun-facing inclined window (Figure 5.7). As long as the two angles of inclination are well chosen, nearly all of the direct and diffuse solar radiation striking the reflector will be reflected through the window. Ground- or roof-reflected radiation reaching the reflector will be lost. An accurate estimate of the solar gain from this type of reflector requires a detailed calculation, but a rough estimate can be obtained by treating the aperture subtended by the window and reflector as an inclined window. This reflector can boost solar gain through the window by about 30%. In a case where 50% of normal window solar gain is lost by heat loss through the window, then the net solar gain is boosted from 50 to 80%, a relative increase of 60%. The overhead reflector also acts as a summer overhang to reduce summer solar gain. This reflector can be designed to look very attractive and can become an integral part of the building.

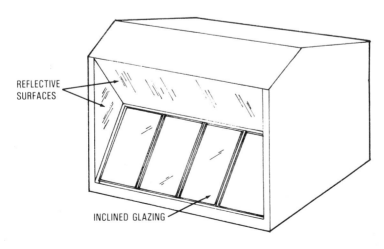

REFLECTIVE SURFACES

INCLINED GLAZING

FIG. 5.7. Inclined reflector above south window

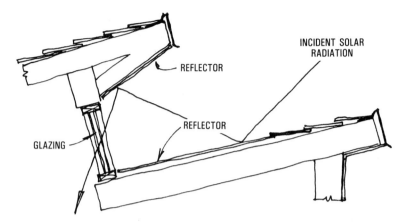

FIG. 5.8. Clerestory window with double reflector

In a clerestory window, the overhead reflector can be combined with a bottom reflector on the roof below the window to provide an extra increase in solar gain (Figure 5.8). In winter, the bottom reflector will be covered in snow in some climates, and will become less effective.

Ground or standard roof reflection increases total solar radiation by up to about 8%, depending on the surface. When covered with snow, the reflected component may be increased to about 25%. Calculations of solar radiation intensities allow for this reflected component, but of course some assumptions about ground *albedo* must be made that may not be satisfied in practice.

Fire Hazard Warning

Reflectors can be plane or curved, or several inclined plane sections may be used. The use of curved or multisection mirrors can provide extra solar gain, but caution is required, and it should never be done without a careful analysis of the reflected radiation. Use of a single plane reflector can never boost the local solar intensity at any place inside the building by more than double. Multisection plane or curved reflectors may increase the local intensity by a large factor, and create a fire hazard.

CHAPTER 6

Thermal Mass Components

MATERIALS

The meaning and significance of thermal mass have been discussed earlier. A building with a glazed area more than 7% of floor area will probably need extra thermal mass above that contained in a normal building structure. Some designers have provided this extra thermal mass as a masonry or water wall immediately opposite the solar windows, or as concrete floors. This type of solar wall can absorb direct solar radiation, but only the outer few centimeters are very effective in storing the solar heat. In midwinter, a floor receives rather low direct solar intensities, due to the low angle of the sun. The floor can, however, receive high intensities if an overhead reflector/window configuration is being used, because the radiation from the reflector strikes the floor at a high angle. Generally, it is advisable to distribute thin layers of thermal mass over the entire inside surface of the solar-heated parts of a building. Extra thickness of drywall or plaster is an ideal way of doing this.

Many buildings have large amounts of thermal mass in the foundations and in the ground around the foundations. Unfortunately, this thermal mass is usually too remote from the main living spaces inside a building to be very effective in storing solar heat. However, if the underground parts of the building are main occupied spaces, as in an underground building, then these large thermal masses can be very useful. These points will be illustrated quantitatively in Part 2.

SOLAR WALL

A solar wall of less than full ceiling height, near the center of a solar-heated space, is another effective thermal mass component (Figure 6.1). It provides thermal storage on both sides of the wall. The space on the far side of the wall receives less direct sunshine, but still-adequate light over the top of the wall, and some people will find this situation more comfortable and congenial.

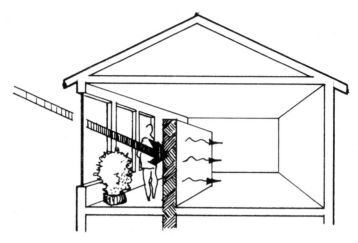

FIG. 6.1. Interior solar wall

TROMBE WALL

Generally, the Trombe wall, shown in Figure 6.2 and described in chapter 4, is an effective way of using masonry because it reaches higher temperatures than in the inside of the building. However, the hottest masonry is not well insulated from the outside, so that the Trombe wall does not utilise solar energy very effectively, nor does it provide a good return on the capital cost of the glazing. It is one of the most effective ways of providing nearly uniform temperatures in a passive solar design, and avoids direct sunshine inside the building. Simplified quantitative assessments of Trombe walls are discussed in some detail in Part 2.

PHASE-CHANGE MATERIALS

A number of commercial phase-change materials are available in the form of rods, translucent pods, steel cans, and plastic trays or pouches. A specially formulated calcium chloride hexahydrate with a phase change at 27°C is now being offered in rods

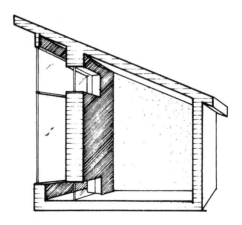

FIG. 6.2. Trombe wall

(Thermol 81), translucent pods (Kalwell), and steel cans (Texxor). Proprietary-treated sodium sulphate decahydrate with phase change at 32°C is being sold in pouches (Heat Pac) or plastic trays (Saskatchewan Minerals). Some currently available phase-change materials are shown in Fig. 6.3.

Figure 6.3a is a wall panel designed to fit between normal stud spacings at 40 or 60 cm centers. It contains a propriety formulation of calcium chloride hexahydrate. Figure 6.3b is an energy tube containing an unspecified phase-change material, which can have phase-change temperatures ranging from 15 to 32°C. It has nylon ring spaces at each end to permit stacking and air circulation. Figure 6.3c is a phase-change tray, containing sodium sulphate.

Most of these materials have phase-change temperatures ranging from 21 to 27°C. When used inside a living space, this temperature ideally should be just 2 to 3° above the comfort temperature required in a building space. If the phase-change temperature is too low, it is difficult to provide enough material surface area to achieve suffi-

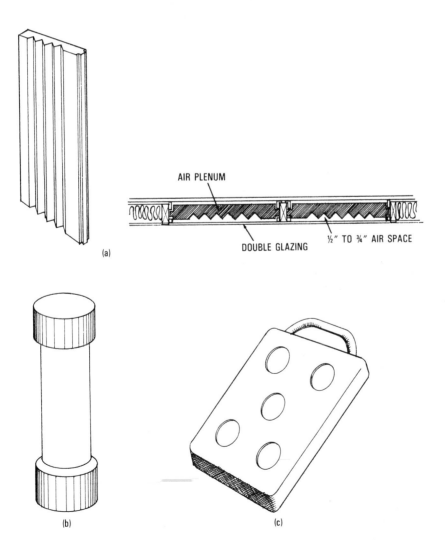

FIG. 6.3. Commercial phase change materials: (a) wall panel in place between wall studs; (b) energy tube; (c) phase-change trays

cient natural heat transfer between the material and building interior; if it is too high, overheating of the building interior will occur. When using phase-change thermal storage, it is important to provide both adequate thermal mass and adequate surface area.[25]

Through the mid-1980s, phase-change materials have not been much used in passive solar buildings. If they are used in the future, it will probably be in innovative designs in which the thermal storage is partially insulated from the main living space. For this use, fairly high phase-change temperatures, around 30–40°C, are desirable.

OTHER MEANS OF THERMAL STORAGE

Various other methods of storing heat have been and are being studied.[26] Some of them offer great promise for storing large amounts of heat in small volumes at relatively low temperatures. If any of these methods are developed commercially, they may have an impact on passive solar design, but seem more likely to be used in large-scale applications rather than in individual houses.

[25]For a discussion of the problems in using phase-change storage efficiently see C. Carter, Phase-change storage in passive solar home heating. *Solar World Forum Proceedings* 3, 1920–1925 (1982). For a description of a recent commercial product see Jerry Germer, Phase-change drywall. *Solar Age* 11(4), 24–27 (1986).

[26]See, for example, G. DeMaria *et al.*, Thermochemical storage of solar energy with high-temperature chemical reactions. *Solar Energy* 35, 409–416 (1985).

PART 2

Quantitative Principles

CHAPTER 7

Overview

A detailed accurate simulation of a passive solar building is necessarily a complex and time-consuming task. Temperature variations and heat flows in the building depend on the thermal properties of the building structure, the varying meteorological environment of the building, and the internal heat sources within the building. The life-style of the building occupants is also relevant, involving such factors as thermostat settings and the opening of doors, windows, and drapes. When all the relevant data have been assembled, they must be fed into a complex computer program that realistically models the heat transfer processes, not only in the building, but in the air and earth surrounding the building.

A number of such simulation packages have been developed, but they are intrinsically research tools, not suitable for day-to-day use by practical building designers. Even as research tools, these packages have their limitations, for it is exceedingly difficult to be sure that the enormous quantity of data assembled really do correspond to an actual building. The effect of occupants' life-style on building performance is a further complication, because it makes it impossible to describe a building's energy properties independently of its occupants.

For practical design purposes, two broadly different approaches are possible. Detailed simulations for a range of buildings in different locations may be used to produce simplified design aids in the forms of tables, graphs, or microcomputer programs. This approach has been extensively developed by the Los Alamos Solar Group, and has many adherents, but we do not recommend it for several reasons. The main problem is its inflexibility. The originators of the design aid must decide what the important design parameters are. Any designer who thinks other parameters are important will find it difficult, if not impossible, to use that particular design aid. Another problem is that such a design aid ignores the basic physical principles underlying passive solar design. Adherence to a simplified design aid outside its range of validity is a possible source of serious design errors. According to Peter Lunde,[27]

---

[27]Peter Lunde, The trouble with SLR — Ignoring theory could dead-end innovative solar design. *Solar Age* **10**, 80 (1980). K. R. Olson, Comparison of solar load ratio predictions with performance of five passive solar buildings. *Intersol 85 Proceedings* **2**, 935–939 (1986) finds very large discrepancies between SLR predictions and actual performance.

the landmark solar load ration (SLR) method has outlived its useful life. Instead of building one of the 94 fixed systems the SLR method defines, architects, engineers, and designers have stubbornly gone on to develop better ones. . . . The 94 SLR designs are now just 94 out-of-date systems.

The second approach to practical passive solar design is to use a simplified calculation method that is firmly based on physical principles but gives up any pretension to predict accurately how any particular building will perform. In view of the normal variations in climatic and thermal properties of building structures and in occupant life-styles, such accurate predictions are impractical anyway outside the research laboratory. However, a good simplified calculation method should be able to give fairly accurate relative predictions. It should, for example, be able to say how much energy saving will come from adding insulation to a building wall, or from putting in a new south-facing window, or from installing a night setback thermostat.

It is also possible to mix the two above approaches. For example, the HOTCAN program, developed by the National Research Council of Canada, calculates steady-state temperatures and heat losses in the conventional way described in chapter 8, but uses the results of detailed studies to include the effects of passive solar gain, rather than computing temperature variations explicitly. The mixed approach can be useful within its range of applicability. HOTCAN works well on energy-efficient building designs with significant, but not dominant, solar gain, but it cannot be used for designs using innovative methods for moving or storing solar heat.

In the following chapters, a number of simple analytic concepts and the simplified calculation methods that arise from them will be described. Their range of application and a comparative assessment of them all will be given. Finally, some microcomputer programs that implement the various methods and some examples of their use will be discussed.

Passive solar systems have several features that often make it realistic to use simple mathematical models to describe them. First, temperature differences within a building are usually small, and heat transfer can be taken to be proportional to these temperature differences. This so-called *linear model* is much easier to use computationally than a nonlinear model, in which rates of heat transfer depend on temperature in a more complicated way. Conventional building heat-loss calculations always use not only a linear model, but a *steady-state* one, in which temperatures do not change with time.

In linear models, the heat transfer across a medium is taken to be proportional to the temperature difference and to the cross-sectional area of the medium. The constant of proportionality is $1/R$, where R is the so-called thermal resistance of the medium. R is strictly defined only when the heat transfer is by conduction, but the three mechanisms of heat transfer — conduction, convection, and radiation — are commonly lumped into this single parameter R, even when convection and radiation are the dominant effects, as in the air spaces between the panes of a double-glazed window. Sometimes the distinctive properties of convective heat flow are allowed for by using different R values for upward, downward, and horizontal heat flow.

Nonlinear effects can be included in both passive and active solar calculations. The standard method of calculating heat losses for active solar collectors due to Duffie and Beckman[28] treats convective and radiative losses as nonlinear, and uses an *iterative* mathematical technique to obtain the temperatures and heat flows in various

[28]J. A. Duffie and W. A. Beckman, *Solar Energy Thermal Processes*. Wiley, New York, 1974.

parts of the collector. In practice, even with collector plates at 80°C above ambient, the second iteration usually produces only a small correction to the first values calculated, thus indicating that a linear model would be adequate in most cases. For passive systems, the smaller temperature differences make a linear model even more reliable; this model should certainly be used in any simplified calculation method.

Another useful property of passive systems is that the building structure usually can be fairly definitely divided into thermal storage material and thermal insulation material. Heavy building materials, such as concrete and brick, and to a lesser extent, wood, have high thermal mass but low thermal resistance, whereas light air-filled materials are good insulators, but have low thermal capacity. It is therefore often possible to develop a simple and realistic mathematical model of a passive solar system in which the insulation materials have thermal resistance but no thermal capacity, while the structural materials have capacity but no resistance. Any small thermal resistance of a structural material may reasonably be included in that of adjacent insulation material. This approach avoids the numerical solution of partial difference–differential equations. Such solutions present no great problems with modern computers, but they are too time-consuming to be repeated many times as part of an engineering design study.

When a building is modeled in this way, by a *thermal network* consisting of a number of points (called *nodes*) joined together by lines (called *arcs*), the thermal masses are allocated to the nodes and the thermal resistances to the arcs. If the capacities and resistances are actually closely coupled, then a very large network may be needed to provide an adequate model of the building. The property discussed in the previous paragraph indicates that the separation of thermal capacity and resistance is often realistic, and quite small network models may give satisfactory results.

The steady-state model used in conventional heat-loss calculations might seem quite inappropriate for passive solar design purposes because solar intensity varies with season and time of day. Variations in temperatures and heat flows are a necessary feature of a passive system. However, these variations are roughly cyclic, that is, after a certain period of time, conditions are approximately the same as at the beginning. The most obvious natural cycles are the daily and annual ones, but we may also study other cycles, such as a few-day one, consisting of a sunny day followed by one or more cloudy days.

The importance of the cycle in passive simulations is that when all thermal resistances are constant over a complete cycle in a linear model, the overall thermal behaviour is given by a steady-state model using the cycle average heat inputs.[29] For example, the total heat flow through a Trombe wall over a cycle is very easily calculated (see chapter 9, Eqn. 9.1). It does not depend on the detailed variations of solar input, ambient or internal temperatures, nor on the thermal mass of the wall. A consequence of this "cycle theorem" is that any simulation method that treats the steady-state problem correctly will predict the overall heat flow correctly even though it may not describe the detailed time variation very adequately.

In practice, the conditions of this theorem are never precisely satisfied. Heat transfer is not linear with constant coefficients. One day is always somewhat different from the next in temperatures, solar radiation, interior building heat gain, and so

---

[29]The cycle average theorem was discussed by Philip Niles in the first *U.S. National Passive Solar Conference Proceedings*, American Section of International Solar Energy Society, Boulder, CO, 1974, pp. 183–188; and by C. Carter in Paper 7-1-3, *Proceedings of Solar Energy Society of Canada*, Solar Energy Society of Canada, Ottawa, 1978. It follows directly from cycle averaging of the linear differential or partial-differential equations governing the heat transfer process.

forth, so strictly diurnal cycles never occur. With all these provisos, however, the linear periodic cycle is often sufficiently close to reality to provide a useful approximation to building behaviour, particularly in cold winter climates, where winter solar overheating is rarely a serious problem in a well-designed building. In milder climates, winter venting may sometimes be needed to avoid overheating. When thermal resistances are frequently changed in this manner, the constant resistance steady-state model becomes less useful.

The cycle theorem just discussed applies only when all thermal resistances are constant. However, we have seen previously that an effective method of improving the performance of a passive solar system is to move insulation to cover the major glazed areas at night. This is particularly true for a Trombe wall, which reaches higher temperatures than most other passive system components. A steady-state model can provide useful information even in this case. We shall see in chapter 9 that when movable insulation is used, net heat flow through the Trombe wall is no longer independent of wall thermal mass, but increases with it, and a steady-state model with infinite thermal mass gives a useful upper limit on the possible heat flow through the wall.

Another useful passive solar principle involves the concept of system *time constants*. All the various heat transfer modes within a passive system have their own time constant. An energy-efficient building, for example, has one long time constant for the escape of heat to ambient, together with a number of shorter time constants for the movement of heat within the building. The actual calculation of system time constants does involve some sophisticated mathematics, but it is well within the capability of modern microcomputers. Although a nonmathematical passive designer may not understand how the time constants are calculated, he or she can appreciate their significance. If, for example, the movement of heat from a thermal storage wall into a living space has a time constant of only a few hours, then it is unrealistic to expect that wall to store solar heat over a cloudy spell of several days' duration, no matter how much solar radiation may impinge upon the wall while the sun is shining.

A detailed passive solar simulation provides an enormous amount of information about temperature variations and heat flows in different parts of the building. Most of this information is quite useless to the building designer, and any simplified simulation method will attempt, as far as possible, to produce only useful information. Although different designers might have slightly different information requirements, the present authors believe that there would be general agreement about the more important requirements. Perhaps the most important is the overall seasonal heating and cooling loads and how these might vary as various design parameters are changed. The next most important requirement might be performance in extreme conditions. What is the peak auxiliary heating needed in extreme winter conditions? Does the building overheat in summer, or even during a mild sunny spell in winter? The analytic methods we shall discuss in the next few chapters have the potential to answer these and similar questions in a fairly simple way.

Part 2 of this book concludes with a description of four computer programs that implement some of the recommended analytic methods. These are all BASIC programs that run in a few seconds on the 8-bit and 16-bit microcomputers currently available. Full listing and documentation for each program is provided.

CHAPTER 8

Conventional Steady-State Heat Loss Calculations

Standard methods have been developed by professional and trade associations to calculate the peak and seasonal heating loads of conventional buildings. The present chapter will summarise the methods recommended by the American Society of Heating and Refrigeration Engineers (ASHRAE) in the *ASHRAE Handbook of Fundamentals*,[30] and will critically assess these methods to see how suitable they are for energy-efficient buildings that have a significant passive solar component.

Calculation of the seasonal heating load follows a procedure that first determines the building's peak heating load, which is the sum of the transmission and infiltration losses plus any additional heat required to handle "pick-up" loading, for example, when thermostat setback is practiced and extra heat is required to bring the building back up to a comfortable temperature. Any steady internal heat gain from people or small appliances is subtracted from the sum to give the final peak load.

HEAT TRANSMISSION LOSSES

Heat transmission losses are calculated as follows. An indoor comfort temperature is chosen and the outdoor *design temperature*, or normal seasonal low temperature, is selected from climatic data available in a table. The *heat transfer coefficients* for walls, glass, ceilings, and floors are selected from tables. ASHRAE gives these values for most standard building materials. The net areas of all walls, glass, and doors adjacent to the outside are determined from building plans or by actual measurement of inside dimensions. The transmission heat losses through each type of surface are then calculated by multiplying the heat transfer coefficient by the net area by the appropriate indoor to outdoor temperature difference (TD).

Calculations of transmission heat losses from the basement are done in a similar manner but with two differences. Where wall areas are below grade the outdoor tem-

[30]*ASHRAE Handbook 1981 Fundamentals*, American Society of Heating, Refrigerating, and Air-Conditioning Engineers, Atlanta, GA, 1981.

perature used is slightly higher because the heat capacity of the soil is taken into consideration. For basement floors, the total perimeter of the slab is used instead of net area, on the assumption that most heat loss occurs through a 1 m wide strip around the perimeter of the slab. In practice, tabulated values are often used for both basement walls and floors. These give the corrected heat transfer coefficients to be used at a particular depth below grade and are then used directly in the standard calculation of losses.

Surface Resistances

The heat loss to a surface due to natural convection and radiation can be represented approximately by a surface thermal resistance. This surface resistance is simply added to the composite resistance of the wall or roof to give the overall thermal resistance R ($= 1/U$). Although the surface resistances are incorporated into the ASHRAE transfer coefficients, it is useful, when the simulation of the Trombe wall is presented, to know how these values are arrived at. The standard ASHRAE values for a nonreflective surface in still air are given in Table 8.1.

When air is being moved over a surface by a wind or fan, there is a forced convection transmittance added to the natural transmittances, equivalent to 3.5 W/($m^2 \times °C$) for every one msec of air speed over the surface.

Example. 5 msec forced convection over a vertical surface

Forced transmittance	$= 5 \times 3.5 = 17.5$	W/($m^2 \times °C$)
Natural transmittance	$= 1/0.12 = 8.3$	W/($m^2 \times °C$)
Total surface transmittance	$= 25.8$	W/($m^2 \times °C$)
Total surface resistance $= 1/25.8 = 0.039$	($m^2 \times °C$)/W

It must be emphasized that this is only an approximate method of calculating heat transfer rates from surfaces. In problems where the heat transfer process is critical, a detailed analysis of convective and radiative processes is required.

INFILTRATION LOSSES

Infiltration losses are the heat losses through cracks around windows, doors, and other joints in the building envelope. These losses are calculated in one of two ways. The first method uses tabulated values that give air leakage for particular wind velocity and type of window or door. The unit value selected is then multiplied by the length of the crack and the temperature difference involved. The product of these calculations times the specific heat of air is the infiltration loss.

The second method, known as the air-change method, is more commonly used. Tables give standard factors that are based on the number of air changes in the space

TABLE 8.1. Surface Resistances

Surface orientation	Direction of heat flow	Surface resistance (W/($m^2 \times °C$))
Horizontal	upward	0.11
Horizontal	downward	0.16
Vertical		0.12

per hour. This factor is typically 0.5, but can vary from 50 to 100% due to extratight houses, poor sealing, unusual winds, and other factors. This factor is then multiplied by the volume (m^3) of the room, the volume specific heat of air ($C_v = 0.33$ Whr/ m$^3 \times$ °C) and by the indoor to outdoor temperature difference to give the infiltration loss. It is convenient to devise an infiltration heat transfer coefficient based on this equation as follows:

$$U_{\text{inf}} = (AC \times C_v \times V)/A \ ,$$

where AC is air changes per hour, V is the volume of the space, and A is the net interior to exterior surface area. This coefficient is multiplied by A and TD in the same manner as the heat transmission coefficient to give infiltration losses.

PICK-UP LOAD

The pick-up loading required in residential buildings depends on factors such as amount of setback, furnace capacity, and inside-to-outside temperature difference. ASHRAE offers only a general guideline that, for 5°C night setback, the heating system should be oversized by 40% to allow for the pick-up load.

ANNUAL HEATING LOAD

When the peak loading has been calculated, an estimate can then be made of the annual heat consumption. The most common method for determining annual heating load is the degree-day procedure. On the assumption that solar and internal gains will offset any heat loss when the mean daily temperature is 18°C, this method estimates the energy required as proportional to the difference between the mean daily temperature and 18°C. For example, if the mean temperature is 10° below 18°C, the fuel consumed is twice as much as on days when the mean temperature is 5°C below 18. Values of degree days per month are published by national metereological offices for many locations around the world. The equation below represents this concept that energy consumed is directly proportional to the number of degree days in the time period considered.

Annual heating load equals:

$$[(H_L) \times (D) \times (24) \times (C_D)]/[(TD) \times (k)] \ ,$$

where

H_L = calculated peak load,

D = number of degree days (from the tables),

C_D = correction factor for heating effect (from the graph in *ASHRAE Handbook of Fundamentals*, page 28.3),

TD = inside/outside temperature difference,

k = correction factor for efficiency rating (e.g., electrical heating = 1; gas heating = 0.55).

In actual calculation of heating loads the following points should be noted: the temperature difference used is always the inside comfort temperature minus the normal low winter ambient temperature, called the "design temperature," and the air change factor for basements is typically half that of upstairs spaces.

Example

The following example gives a typical set of values used to find the annual heating consumption, in kW/hr, of a one-story house. All units are SI. The house is 15.5 m by 8.5 m and has frame construction with a heated, full basement. The foundation slab is 1.5 m below grade and all rooms are 2.4 m in height. The windows are double glazed with wooden frames and the doors are all wood panel type.

The heat transfer coefficients (U) are in W/(m^2 × °C) and were obtained from the ASHRAE handbook. All areas (A) are expressed in square meters. They are the net (inside) surface areas exposed to the outside. The temperature difference (TD) used is 45°C and is based on an inside comfort temperature of 21°C and a design temperature of −24°C. The air-change factor is 0.5 changes per hour for upstairs and 0.25 for the basement.

Annual Heating Load

In this example the heating load (H_L) is the 14.0 kW peak load calculated in Table 8.2. The degree day value (D) and appropriate C_D from tables are 4600 and 0.65, respectively. The temperature difference (TD) is 45. The efficiency factor (k) as given for electrical heating is 1.

$$[(14.0)(4600)(24)(0.65)]/[(45)(1)] = 22,400 \text{ kWhr} \ .$$

CONCLUSION

It is clear from the previous description that the standard heat-loss calculation methods involve many dubious and arbitrary assumptions. They can lead to inaccurate estimation in areas where unusual temperature distribution or climatic conditions occur. Also, the degree-day tables were compiled before any serious attempt was made to increase furnace efficiency or insulation levels. But it is in the calculation of peak loading that much of the error occurs. As mentioned previously, the

TABLE 8.2. Peak Heating Load

	U	A	Losses (W)
Transmission Losses*			
Main floor			
Walls	0.40	82.0	1476
Glass	2.64	40.0	4752
Doors	1.88	3.9	324
Ceiling	0.20	120.0	1080
Basement floor and walls			
Wall above grade	0.56	50.0	1266
Wall below grade	0.25	56.0	630
Slab	0.15	132.0	891
Infiltration Losses†			
Main floor	0.21	246.0	2348
Basement	0.11	238.0	1178
Total Losses			13945
Peak Load (kW)			14.0

* = ($U \times A \times TD$)
† = ($U_{inf} \times A \times TD$)

maximum inside to outside temperature difference is always used. When the heated space is adjacent to an unheated, interior space or to an exterior masonry wall heated by the sun, the temperature difference used should be considerably less. For example, the losses through ceilings are not modified, even though there may be an insulating attic space above. The heat transfer coefficients for glass represent maximum peak loading and do not take into consideration any off-setting solar gain. In general, the whole area of pick-up loading for residential buildings is poorly addressed. The guidelines overestimate extra load requirements, particularly where newer furnaces are used and thermostat setback is on an automatic timer. Furthermore, the guidelines completely ignore any energy savings from the setback itself. And although internal gain is nearly always significant, it is rarely taken into account when calculations are made of the peak loading.

The conventional methods do not adequately address the effects of passive solar gain, the storage of heat in the building structure, or the situation when different parts of the building are maintained at different temperatures.

CHAPTER 9

Nonconventional Steady-State Calculations

ZONED STEADY-STATE CALCULATIONS

Conventional heat-loss calculations discussed in the previous chapter assume that the whole building will be kept at the same constant temperature so there is no heat flow from one part of the building to another. It is now becoming recognised that this is not what many building occupants really want. In residences, many people prefer their bedrooms to be cooler than their sitting areas, and other rooms could also be cooler without any significant loss of comfort. This concept of keeping different parts of a building at different temperatures is sometimes called "zoning."

When some zones are cooler than others, heat will flow from the warmer zones to the cooler ones. This means that the cooler zones will always have a smaller heating load than calculated by the conventional methods, and during the milder parts of the heating season may not have any heating load at all. For calculation purposes, zoning requires a knowledge of the thermal transmittances between the different zones. In so far as the zones are separated by fixed partitions, these conductances may be determined by the methods discussed in the last chapter. Often, however, there may be doors and windows that can be opened between zones, and the steady-state calculation must make some assumptions about the proportion of time these are open. Zoning will provide the maximum gains in energy efficiency if interzone doors are kept closed as much as possible.

Calculation of steady-state zone temperatures requires the numerical solution of a set of linear equations (Appendix A, "Steady-State Network Model"), with one equation for each zone. As long as the different temperatures are constant in time, we still have a steady-state problem, which can be solved by an extension of the conventional steady-state methods. This is trivial mathematically as long as the number of zones is not too large, and a microcomputer program, ZONESTEAD, to do this for up to 10 zones is included in chapter 12.

Example

The example that illustrates steady-state zoning is a simulation of the Saunders' sandwich house, using monthly averages for solar radiation and ambient temperatures when no fans are operating. The model is described more fully in chapter 10, where we give a time-varying simulation of this design. The computer results for the steady-state model are given in chapter 12 under ZONESTEAD. The building interior, zone 3, has a uniform 1000 W internal gain, but no auxiliary heat. The results show that the interior is maintained at an average temperature of 19°C in the coldest months of December and January and would be too hot in other months without the use of a fan.

THE STEADY STATE FOR A TROMBE WALL

As we have discussed earlier, the actual temperature variations through a Trombe wall can be very complicated. In particular, the outside surface temperature varies very rapidly if the impinging solar insolation varies rapidly, as it may well do, due to cloud movement. Even the most sophisticated simulation procedures cannot hope to follow such rapid temperature variations, but fortunately it is not necessary. Rapid variations at the surface do not have any significant effect on the overall heat transmitted through the wall.

If all the thermal transmittances are constant throughout a cycle, the total heat flow through the wall over the cycle is given by the steady-state temperature distribution with a cycle average for the solar insolation, ambient temperature, and interior temperature. The steady-state temperature through a wall is a very simple linear variation between the outside and inside surfaces, and the average heat flow through the wall is

$$q = (T_a + QR_0 - T_i)/(R_0 + R_1 + R) \ , \qquad (9.1)$$

where Q, R, and T denote solar insolation, thermal resistance, and temperature, respectively; suffices 0 and 1 denote outside and inside wall surfaces, a denotes ambient; i denotes interior; and R, without suffix, is the thermal resistance of the wall itself. The derivation of this equation is found in Appendix A.

The above steady-state value for average heat flow is realistic for any Trombe wall without night insulation over the outside glazing. It does not, of course, predict daily variations in heat flow, which will depend on the thermal mass and thickness of the wall. Other studies have shown that thick masonry walls (45 cm) have very little daily variation in heat flow, whereas thinner walls (10–20 cm) have a peak flow in the evening a few hours after the peak daily solar insolation. With this background knowledge of the general effect of wall thickness, the steady-state average flow formula enables a rapid assessment of Trombe wall performance in any particular location.

Example

The next example of the use of the steady-state model calculates overall heat flows through windows and Trombe walls. Table 9.1 gives the calculated average winter heat flows through a double glazed window and double glazed Trombe walls of thickness 15 and 45 cm, for the 6-month season, November to April, in Ottawa, Canada, using monthly solar radiation data.

The formula requires an estimate of the average interior temperature, T_i, which can only be known from a simulation of the performance of the whole building.

TABLE 9.1. Average Heat Flows, q, Through Windows and Trombe Walls,
W/m² November–April, Ottawa, Canada

Input data

Windows

$$\text{Eqn. (9.1) reduces to } q = Q + U(T_a - T_i)$$

where

$U = 2.75$ W/(m² × °C)
$Q = 99$ W/m²
$ = 130$ W/m² × 0.76 (average insolation × solar transmittance of double glazing)
$T_a = 0$°C

Walls $R_0 = 0.25$ (m² × °C)/W
$R_1 = 0.10$ (m² × °C)/W
$R = 0.36$ (m² × °C)/W (45 cm)
$ = 0.12$ (m² × °C)/W (15 cm)
$Q = 130$ W/m²
$T_a = 0$°C

	Window		Trombe wall	
	no overheat	overheat	15 cm	45 cm
$T_i^* =$	20	22	21	20
$q\dagger =$	44	39	29	21

Note. Overheat: Room is allowed to rise 2 to 22°C to use more solar heat.
* = interior temperature; † = average heat flow.

However, small changes in the T_i will not affect the result very much. The values of T_i used are indicated.

The formula and Table 9.1 show immediately, without any elaborate calculations, that a window transmits more heat than a Trombe wall, and a thinner wall more than a thicker one. In a cold December, this heat flow may be a loss, as it is in Ottawa, but over the entire heating season there is a net gain as shown.

THE TROMBE WALL — EFFECT OF MOVABLE INSULATION

When movable insulation is used to reduce night heat losses, the net heat flow through the wall into the building interior increases with the thermal capacity C for the following reasons.[31] All time constants are proportional to C, so temperature variations are smoothed out as C increases. In particular, with a higher C, the outside wall surface temperature is lower during the solar heating part of the cycle (day) and higher at night. Thus, the heat losses to ambient from the outer wall surface would be lower by day and higher by night, but with constant thermal resistance, the overall cycle heat loss is unaffected. However, if night insulation is used, the night heat losses are reduced, so the overall result of a higher thermal capacity is a net reduction in heat loss from the wall surface, and hence an increase in the heat flow through the wall.

---

[31]C. Carter, *Heat Conduction through the Trombe Wall.* Paper 80-Ht-22 presented at the Joint ASME/AIChE National Heat Transfer Conference, Orlando, FL, April, 1980.

TABLE 9.2. Daily Heat Flows Through a Trombe Wall: A—Insolation Constant over 8 hr day; B—Insolation Peaked at Midday

Input Data			
Resistances (in $m^2 \times °C/W$):			
Glazing	R^0	0.25	
Movable insulation	R^2	2.25	
Wall	R	0.25	
Inside wall surface	R^i	0.10	
Wall thermal capacity	C	200 Whr/m$^2 \times °C$)	
Internal temperature	T^i	20°C	
Night ambient temperature		0°C	
Cycle period		24 hr	
Dry solar insolation (Q; in W/m^2)	A	B	hr
	400	200	(0–1, 7–8)
	400	400	(1–2, 6–7)
	400	500	(2–6)

Output Data

A		B	
Time (hr)	Heat flow (W/m^2)	Time (hr)	Heat flow (W/m^2)
4	51	6	51
8	57	10	63
16	67	16	67

	Daily Totals (Whr/m^2)	
1435	with insulation	1425
1559	infinite capacity	1559
533	without insulation	533

An upper bound for the heat flow through the wall is obtained by letting the thermal mass become indefinitely large. Then there are no temperature time variations at all. Heat flows into the wall are then controlled by the thermal transmittances $(1/R)$, and hence the upper bound for overall heat flow through the wall is given by a steady-state temperature distribution using cycle averages for solar insolation and ambient temperature, and transmittances.

Detailed simulations[32] indicate that this upper bound is often approached quite closely with practically realisable walls. The formula for the upper bound heat flow is the same as that given above, but with R_0 replaced by $1/U_0$, where the thermal conductance U is the reciprocal of the thermal resistance R and U_0 is the value of the outside surface transmittance U_0 averaged over the cycle.

$$\text{So:} \quad q = (T_a + Q/U_0 - T_i)/(1/U_0 + R_1 + R) \ . \tag{9.2}$$

Table 9.2 gives the heat flows through a Trombe wall and the daily totals in Whr/m^2 over a 24-hr cycle. Examples A and B differ only in that insolation in A is constant at 400 W/m^2 over an 8-hr day, whereas in B it varies from 200 W/m^2 in the morning to 500 at noon. Generally, example B would be more realistic, but

---

[32]Results on daily variation of heat flow through a Trombe wall have been given by various authors, for example, E. Mazria, *The Passive Solar Energy Book*. Rodale, Emmaus, PA, 1979, p. 164.

Table 9.2 shows that the time distributions make very little difference to the behaviour of the Trombe wall. This example also illustrates the effectiveness of movable night insulation. When such insulation is in place, the total cycle heat flow is about 85% of the infinite capacity limit, whereas without insulation the daily flow is only about 35% of this limit.

Other strategies are sometimes recommended for improving the performance of a Trombe wall by use of varying thermal resistances. The most common one is the insertion of vents at the top and bottom of the wall with controllable dampers or fans to transfer solar heat more quickly into the interior of the building. It is possible to develop other steady-state models that approximate the average heat flow in these circumstances. However, because none of these strategies improve the Trombe wall performance appreciably, these models will not be discussed.

CHAPTER 10

Time Variations of Temperatures and Heat Flows

It was noted in the previous chapters that a surprisingly large amount of useful information can be obtained from simple steady-state calculations, but sometimes it is desirable to know how temperatures and heat flows change with time in various parts of a building. A network model, as described in chapter 7, is convenient for computing time variations, and is used in most of the large research simulation packages. A discussion of time variation is necessarily more mathematical, but we have as far as possible relegated most of the mathematics to Appendix B.

Once a network model has been constructed, the usual research approach has been to use a finite difference numerical method to solve the differential equations that define the time-varying temperatures at each node. The derivation of these equations is given in Appendix A. A common approach is to run a simulation for a typical year, using hour by hour meteorological data that are made available on magnetic tape by the national meteorological offices. The complexity of these procedures is immediately obvious, but there are more fundamental reasons why it is difficult to transfer these research procedures from the laboratory to the design office. The heat transfer *differential equations* have a property that has become known in the numerical analysis community as "stiffness." In simple terms, this means that any change in the heat inputs to the network causes rapid transient changes in the temperatures. The solution of stiff differential equations is still an active field of research in numerical analysis, but one normal requirement is the use of small time steps during transient periods. The problem of stiffness makes it difficult to produce simple robust *finite difference* simulation packages for designers.

There are some alternatives to finite difference simulations. One is the response factor method used in the American DOE2 and the Canadian ENCORE packages.[33] To

---

[33]The simulation program ENCORE is described in a report NRCC 17663 from the National Research Council of Canada, 1978.

the authors' knowledge, this method has never been transferred out of the research laboratory.

The alternative that we prefer for simplified linear simulations is the modal method, usually called the spectral method by mathematicians. This starts from a steady-state temperature distribution, as discussed in chapter 9. Temperature variations from the steady state are included by adding to the steady-state temperature a series of time-decaying transient "modes," which decay ever more rapidly as we move up the series. A mode is actually a spatial temperature configuration multiplied by an exponentially decaying time term. As the most transient modes decay, the overall temperature distribution in the network gradually approaches the steady-state distribution. The transients are the same ones that cause the problems in finding finite difference solutions. In the modal method, the most rapidly decaying transients simplify the problem, for they can often be neglected altogether. The number of modes actually used in a simulation depends on the importance of temperature variation in a particular application, and the degree of detail required in the model.

Perhaps we should pause to consider the different meanings of the similar-sounding words, mode and node. A node is a component of a heat transfer network in which thermal mass is located, and which represents some physically distinct part of a building. A mode is a term in the series representation of the temperature variations at the nodes. Mathematically the modes are the *eigenvectors* of the heat transfer matrix, and the modal time constants are the inverse *eigenvalues*. The total number of modes equals the number of nodes in the network, but, depending on the application, it may not be necessary to include the more rapidly decaying modes in order to provide an adequate description of the thermal behaviour of the building.

The computer calculation of the modes and time constants is simple and fast for small networks, but the amount of calculation increases rapidly with the size of network. Studies have actually shown[34] that the modal method is competitive with finite difference methods in computation time for networks with up to several hundred nodes. For the very small networks, with no more than 10 nodes, which we recommend for simplified design simulations, the modal method is usually two to four times faster than finite difference methods, and also has the important robustness property discussed previously.

The modal method can be applied not only to networks, but also to problems in continuous linear heat conduction, as in the Trombe wall, and in fact then reduces to the standard infinite series method for solving such problems. The main novelty in applying the method to the Trombe wall is the demonstration of how few terms from the infinite series need to be included to give extremely accurate results.

A brief description of the mathematics of the modal method is given in Appendix B, together with references to more detailed discussions in the literature. Most readers will probably be content to use the computer programs provided without delving into the mathematics. There are three such programs. One, called WALLSPEC, computes the temperature variations in a wall adjacent to a single temperature node, representing a building interior, according to the standard linear heat conduction equation (Appendix B, "For a Wall"). WALLSPEC should be used for problems in which the dominant heat transfer and storage effects are taking place in a wall, and the rest of the building can be adequately represented by just a single node. The second program, called NETSPEC, computes temperature variations in a network with

---

[34]C. Carter and W. Scholfield, Analytic numerical solutions of a class of stiff linear differential equations with piecewise-constant coefficients. *Congressus Numerantum* **51**, 103–111 (1986).

linear heat transfer, and is recommended for use particularly with innovative passive solar designs. The third program, SUNSPEC, is a general simulation program for energy-efficient buildings with significant passive solar gain, but with no innovative features for the transfer or storage of solar heat. SUNSPEC uses NETSPEC as a subprogram, and uses many of the simulation simplifications discussed in chapter 11. The programs are given in chapter 12.

The nature of the modes and their time constants varies with the type of passive design. A superinsulated house has a principal mode with a long time constant, usually about 2 days. This mode is one in which the temperatures of all parts of the building move together. The other modes, with much shorter time constants of a few hours or less, have widely different temperatures at different nodes, and their contribution to the overall temperature variation is to represent the flow of heat from one part of the building to another. They normally play no significant role in the overall energy performance of the house.

A passive solar design, such as the Saunders' solar sandwich, which aims to provide close to complete solar heating, must have some means of storing solar heat over several days. The building must have at least one modal time constant in excess of 100 hr, and this mode must not involve significant heat storage in the main living space if overheating is to be avoided. The more common direct gain designs, in which solar heat is stored in thermal mass in the living space, can never meet this requirement because transfer of heat from this thermal mass into the living space has a time constant of a few hours at most.

The section that follows illustrates the importance of modal time constants with examples of superinsulated house, direct gain passive solar house, Trombe wall solar house, hot climate unglazed solar wall house, and solar sandwich house. Of these five designs, only the last has the appropriate long time constant mode that indicates the ability to release solar heat over a succession of cold, cloudy days.

SUPERINSULATED DESIGN

This house has 10 m^2 of south window, transmitting 6,000 W of solar radiation for 8 hr on a clear winter day. It has a thermal transmittance of 90 W/°C, a thermal mass of 12.6 MJ/°C, and a uniform internal gain of 1,000 W. The two largest time constants are 40 hr and 15 min. The first governs the mode in which the temperatures of all parts of the building move up and down together, whereas the second represents heat transfer between building structure and interior space.

The house is modeled over a 3-day cycle, with the first day clear, the others cloudy with only diffuse radiation at 1/10 the intensity of the clear day radiation. With ambient temperatures of 0°C by day and −6°C by night, and with no auxiliary heat, the interior temperature rises to 24°C after 8 hr of sunshine, falls to 17 after one day, to 13 after two days, and to 11 after three days. The addition of somewhat more glass or more mass can vary the peak temperature, but has no significant effect on the low temperature after 3 days.

DIRECT GAIN DESIGN

This house has 20 m^2 of south window, a thermal conductance of 150 W/°C, and a uniform internal heat gain of 1,000 W. The thermal storage wall has a conductivity of 0.9 W/m/°C, a thermal capacity of 1.8 MJ/m^3/°C, and a surface thermal transmittance of 10 W/m^2/°C. Apart from the wall, the house has a thermal capacity of 10.8 MJ/°C.

TABLE 10.1. Direct Gain House

Wall		Two longest time constants (hr)		Solar mainly to	Temp (°C)	
area (m²)	thickness				max	min
20	0.15	34	6.9	wall	22	7
				space	27	6
20	0.30	60	11.7	wall	23	8
				space	28	7
40	0.15	46	5.3	wall	22	8
				space	26	7

Table 10.1 gives the two highest time constants for three different storage walls, one 15 cm thick and 20 m² area, another 30 cm thick with 20 m² area, and a third 15 cm thick and 40 m² area. The longest time constant is for the temperature variation of the wall. It is the second one that represents the heat transfer mode between wall and interior. In each case, this time is only a few hours, indicating that the wall cannot store useful solar heat for long periods.

Each case is modeled over the 3-day cycle previously described. The interior temperature rises to a maximum after 8 hr of sunshine, and then falls to a minimum after 3 days. The table gives maximum and minimum temperatures when the solar radiation goes mainly (75%) to the wall, or mainly to the interior space. The results reaffirm that direct sunshine on the storage wall reduces overheating by a few degrees, but has no significant effect on the interior temperature after three days.

The complete WALLSPEC computer printout for the first wall in Table 10.1 is given as a WALLSPEC example in chapter 12.

TROMBE WALL DESIGN

To obtain average interior temperatures over a 3-day cycle comparable to the superinsulated and direct gain designs, 50 m² of 30 cm thick Trombe wall are needed in a house with transmittance (apart from the wall) of 85 W/°C. The wall has a thermal capacity of 27 MJ/°C, the rest of the building 5.4 MJ/°C. The two longest time constants are 50 and 6 hr. Over the 3-day cycle, the interior temperature reaches a peak of 20°C early in the second day, due to the time delay introduced by the Trombe wall. It then drops to 15 after two days and to 12 after three days. As we have seen in the previous section, a thicker wall reduces the temperature variation, but also reduces the average temperature.

Trombe Wall Design with Transparent Insulation

In chapter 5, we discussed the possibility of developing a glazing with high solar transmission and high thermal insulation, a so-called "transparent insulation." The above Trombe wall simulation is repeated with all data unchanged except that the thermal resistance of the glazing has been increased to 1.0 RSI, from 0.4 RSI. The glazing thus has the solar transmission of double glazing, but the thermal insulation of five-pane glazing. Such a glazing is not available currently, but is technically feasible.

The longest time constant is increased to 75 hr, the peak interior temperature is 32°C, and the minimum temperature after three days is 22°C. This indicates that transparent insulation could play a significant role in increasing the amount of solar heat transmitted through a Trombe wall, but it would not have much effect on interior temperature variations over a several day cloudy period.

Because a peak interior temperature of 32°C is unacceptable, the use of transparent insulation would enable and require the area of Trombe wall to be reduced. The steady-state equation (9.1) in chapter 9 can be used to estimate the area of wall required to transmit the same amount of solar energy as the 50 m^2 wall with normal double glazing. Thus, the use of transparent insulation with a Trombe wall would reduce the area of wall and glazing needed, but it would not significantly increase the amount of solar energy that can be used effectively.

HOT-CLIMATE DESIGN WITH SOLAR WALL

This is a well-insulated house with an unglazed, uninsulated thick thermal mass wall on the sun-facing side. The complete computer results for two states are given in chapter 12 under NETSPEC. State 0 is the normal building condition. State 1 is a summer condition in which a vent is opened at night, thus increasing the heat loss to ambient from 160 to 800 W/°C. Because the thermal mass wall is exposed to the ambient, the largest time constant is about 20 hr, indicating that it is unrealistic to expect any temperature smoothing effect over more than 1 day.

Over a mild winter day with ambient temperature between 5 and 10°C, the interior temperature is maintained between 19 and 26°C, with the inside wall surface temperature between 22 and 27°C. Over a hot summer day with ambient temperature between 18 and 30°C, effort is made to screen out direct sunshine and minimise internal gain, and the vent is opened for 12 hr, evening and night. Now the interior temperature remains between 20 and 28°C, and the inside wall surface temperature between 23 and 27°C.

In both winter and summer, the inside wall surface temperature varies less than the interior temperature; so the radiative heat from the wall has a moderating effect and improves the comfort condition over a 24-hr period. However, because of the 20-hr time constant, the moderating effect will not persist when there is no solar gain on a winter day, or no marked drop in ambient temperature on a summer night.

SAUNDERS' SANDWICH DESIGN

None of the standard passive solar designs considered so far have any modal time constants longer than about 2 days, and they are incapable of storing solar heat over long periods. Thicker walls have longer time constants for heat retention in the wall, but this heat is not readily placed into or retrieved from the inside of a thick wall. The Saunders' sandwich design may have a principal time constant of about 5 days, and can provide effectively complete solar heating.

The complete computer results for the simulation of this building are also given in chapter 12 under NETSPEC. With only 20 m^2 of solar glazing, it is possible to maintain satisfactory temperatures over a 4-day cycle (1 sunny, 3 cloudy) with the same ambient temperatures as in the previous 3-day cycle. Without the fan (state 0 in the table), the principal time constant is 127 hours. Two different fan speeds are used in states 1 and 2, with transmittances between attic (node 1) and rocks (node 5) of 10 and 20 W/°C. The interior temperature (node 3) varies between 20 and 26°C over the 4-day cycle.

CHAPTER 11

Simulation Procedures

Simulation models should contain only as much detail as is necessary to explain the building behaviour to the required accuracy. There are several penalties arising from use of an unnecessarily complicated model. Computational complexity increases both in time and in hardware requirements. Perhaps more important is that more input data are required for a more complex model, and often the accuracy of the extra data may not be adequate to justify the use of the complex model. This is particularly true in the design office, where it is not productive to spend much time collecting and verifying data. Another problem with complex models is that they produce large amounts of output, which may be of little use and are in fact often left unanalysed.

The amount of detail used in describing the building depends upon comfort requirements. If the intention is to maintain a uniform temperature throughout the building, then the whole building could reasonably be represented by a single network node, with possibly a few other nodes to represent key structural elements in the building and to simulate the time-delaying effects of structural thermal mass as the ambient temperature changes. If the building is to be zoned, with different zones at different comfort temperatures, there must be at least one node representing each zone, again with extra structural nodes to simulate time delay effects. If some zones will have significant temperature variations due either to passive solar gain or temperature setback, then it is important to introduce extra nodes to represent the main thermal storage structures in the zone. Generally, experience and judgment are needed to select a satisfactory network model. If there is any doubt as to whether a particular building component should be represented by one or more nodes, several different representations may be tried and compared. It should usually be possible to obtain a reasonably reliable simulation with no more than 10 nodes in the network.

When a single structure such as a mass wall is modeled by more than one node, it is most accurate to split it into a number of sections of equal thickness with a node in the middle of each section. The thermal transmittance of each arc is based on the resistance of the material and the distance between nodes, except for the outermost sections, for which surface resistances must be considered.

In addition to the nodes in a network for which the heat sources are specified and the temperatures are to be determined, there will always be a node representing the ambient with a specified temperature. More generally, a network may contain any arbitrary number of nodes with specified temperatures. In addition to the ambient, these might represent building zones maintained at fixed temperatures, or possibly phase-change thermal storage materials, assumed to be held at their phase-change temperatures. Such nodes with specified temperatures will be termed fixed nodes, to distinguish them from the variable nodes for which temperatures are to be computed. The computational complexity of a network problem depends almost entirely on the number of variable nodes, so there is a definite advantage in representing building zones by fixed nodes whenever this is realistic. A zone that is held at a specified temperature some of the time can be represented by a fixed node during that time, and by a variable zone at other times. This flexibility is allowed in the computer program SUNSPEC, but not in the current version of NETSPEC. Once the temperatures of the variable nodes have been computed, a very simple calculation then finds the heat flows into or out of the fixed nodes.

One of the most stringent requirements is the simulation of temperature setback. The main problem occurs during the temperature recovery pick-up period after the setback. If we use too simple a network model, we may find that we are attempting to quickly raise the temperature of a large part of the thermal mass of the building. In practice, however, the air temperature is first raised, then in succession the temperatures of the inner and outer parts of the building structure. Use of too simple a model can grossly overestimate the auxiliary heat needed for temperature recovery.

The simplest type of modal model beyond the steady-state model is the single or principal mode model, in which the temperatures of all parts of the building are assumed to change together. Such a model will arise from a one-node network, in which the whole building is represented by a single node, but it can also occur in a multinode network when the effects of the transient modes are neglected. The principal mode model can be useful in predicting temperature ranges in a building. It cannot adequately describe the effects of thermostat setback or solar heat storage in the building structure. Nor can it handle the subtle smoothing effects when interior building temperatures are held steady, but ambient temperatures vary, because these effects depend essentially on some part of the building structure having a varying temperature.

In the discussion of the Trombe wall, we have indicated that the detailed solar insolation variation on the outside surface of the wall is not very important. The same is true more generally in all energy-efficient passive systems, for both solar insolation and ambient temperature variations. Detailed simulation studies[35] have shown that the temperature smoothing in a well-insulated building renders unimportant the detailed time variations in solar gain and ambient temperature. As long as the broad daily variations are modeled correctly, the energy performance of the house is predicted adequately. The modal method that we recommend can do this ideally; for, unlike finite difference methods, it does not need small time steps to produce stable and accurate numerical solutions. For many purposes, it is adequate to divide a 24-hr day into just two intervals, using average day and night sources and ambient temperatures. This very crude approximation will normally predict overall daily heat flows to within 1% accuracy, and peak heat flows to within 5%.

Two major uncertainties in most simulations are the heat losses due to air infiltration and through the ground. Outside the research laboratory, and sometimes inside

[35]C. D. Barley, *Passive Solar Simulation with Daily Weather Data*. 4th U.S. National Passive Solar Conference, Kansas City, MO, 1979.

it, it is very difficult to establish either a clear relation between building structure and air infiltration or the heat-transfer properties of the earth around a building. These uncertainties are a problem with any type of building, but can be serious in energy-efficient buildings, where these two heat-loss mechanisms are often dominant. As more designs call for controlled air infiltration by fans or an air-to-air heat exchanger, this factor may become more predictable, provided we can be sure that all caulking and air–vapour barrier installation really is done according to specification. For buildings where these two uncertainties are important, the best approach is to run simulations over the range of probable values of air infiltration and ground heat loss.

The transfer of heat between zones by natural convection or use of fans can be approximated by a heat-transfer coefficient in a manner similar to the air-change method for infiltration discussed in chapter 8. An estimate must be made of the rate of air movement (m^3/hr), which is then multiplied by the volume specific heat of air [$C_v = 0.33$ Whr/($m^3 \times °C$)] to yield the thermal transmittance in W/°C. One caveat about the current network model is that it is unable to simulate a closed convection loop involving more than two nodes. Such a convection loop in a building may be approximated by a sequence of two-node loops, as we have done in modeling the Saunders' sandwich in chapter 12.

There is no general agreement about the type of climatological data to be used in simplified simulations. The following suggestions are based on considerable experience, but we recognise that good arguments can be advanced for other approaches. One advantage of three of the general computer programs ZONESTEAD, NETSPEC, and WALLSPEC, described in chapter 12, is that they can accept whatever data the user considers appropriate.

Conventional steady-state heat loss calculations use only two climatological numbers: the total seasonal heating degree days, and the so-called design temperature, the normal lowest winter temperature. This has the advantage of simplicity, and enables estimates to be made of overall seasonal heating load and size of heating system needed to meet peak heating requirements. It also allows simple comparisons to be made with actual heating seasons that may be warmer or colder than normal. However, as discussed in chapter 8, it does not make adequate allowance for passive solar gain or for interior heat gains in buildings where these have dominant effects, nor for the pick-up from temperature setback. We believe it makes sense for simplified passive solar simulations to use as much as possible of the conventional methods and to add only the extra data needed to allow adequately for solar and internal heat gains. We will now consider how this might be done.

The previous considerations suggest that a reasonable simplified simulation can often be developed from the design temperature, the number of months in the heating season, the total degree days in the heating season, and the number of bright sunshine hours in the heating season. In conformity with this data, a number of typical days to simulate should be selected. One day should be a mild, clear day, another should be a cold, sunless day with temperature dropping to the design temperature at night. The other days, or possibly sequence of days, must represent typical average conditions and allow an overall estimate of seasonal heating load. The designer has some flexibility in the choice of typical days that conform with the climatological data.

One requirement in a simulation is to assess the possibility of overheating due to solar gain on a sunny, mild winter day. This can be done by a clear-day simulation. Clear-day solar insolation depends on latitude and time of year; the appropriate data for these variables can be chosen from the reference manuals. However, in most cases it will probably be adequate to use the following very simple procedure. As we move from 32° to 56° latitude north, the time of maximum clear-day insolation on a south-facing vertical surface moves from late December to late March, but the value remains fairly constant between 5.6 and 5.9 kWhr/m^2/day, and the number of sunshine hours varies between 7.2 and 8.0 hr/day. It is therefore reasonably accurate to take the clear day insolation as 700 W/m^2 over an 8-hr day, independent of latitude. For a more accurate simulation, some variation of insolation over the day could be included; it would still be reasonably independent of latitude.

Another important requirement is an assessment of the total seasonal useful solar heat. Average monthly solar insolations are published for many locations, and hours of bright sunshine are available for many more. A study of several widely different locations indicates that generally there is between 650 and 700 W/m^2 average insolation for each hour of bright sunshine during the heating season. There is some evidence that the figure is slightly higher for extreme latitudes,[36] but for most locations, where solar gain can significantly reduce space heating loads, it will often be adequate to use an average solar insolation of 700 W/m^2 on a south-facing vertical surface for every hour of bright sunshine.

The use of bright sunshine hours to determine solar gain is consistent with the detailed studies by John Hay of the University of British Columbia. He has developed correlation formulae that express the average monthly solar radiations on both horizontal and inclined surfaces entirely in terms of bright sunshine hours and surface albedo.

If a building has glazing inclined to the vertical, or with orientations other than to the south, the designer will not be able to use the two simplifications discussed in the last two paragraphs, but will have to use the appropriate numbers from the climatological reference tables or a correlation formula. A microcomputer program, SOLRAD, based on the correlation formulae of Hay and Iqbal described in Appendix C, is given in chapter 12.

Internal heat gains can meet a major part of the heating load in an energy-efficient building. These gains come partly from people and animals, and partly from heat-generating appliances. The total and time distribution of the gains depends very much on the type of building and the life-style of its occupants. In the absence of any definite information about these heat gains, the most reasonable procedure is to take them as constant throughout the heating season. For a home, an appropriate value for this constant is 300 W per occupant. If more detailed information is available, it may be used. Fortunately, for the same reasons we have indicated earlier, the time distribution is not very important.

In chapter 12, we describe an interactive simulation program, SUNSPEC, which uses the ideas presented in this chapter. Unlike the three fundamental programs, ZONESTEAD, WALLSPEC, and NETSPEC, which are based entirely on the scientific principles of heat transfer, SUNSPEC does make a number of assumptions and is to that extent a black-box type of package. The assumptions are described in chapter 12, but they are somewhat involved, and many users might not wish to study them in detail. Generally, SUNSPEC should be adequate for energy-efficient buildings in which passive solar gains are significant but not dominant. It is not recommended for innovative passive solar designs that attempt to provide a major fraction of solar heating. Serious errors can arise if such a package is used in circumstances outside its range of validity.

---

[36]See particularly, J. D. Hay, An analysis of solar radiation data for selected locations in Canada. *Climatological Study Number 32* of Atmospheric Environment Service of Canada, 1977. This shows that solar radiation at Churchill (latitude 59° North) is about 800 W/sq. m for each bright sunshine hour.

CHAPTER 12

Microcomputer Programs

ZONESTEAD

This BASIC program calculates the steady-state temperatures and heat flows in a linear thermal network. The network has N nodes (or zones): M variable nodes with specified heat sources, $Q(I)$, $I = 1$ to M, and F fixed nodes with specified temperatures, $T(J)$, $J = M + 1$ to $M + F (= N)$. The program computes the temperatures for the variable nodes, and the heat flows into the fixed nodes. Any consistent set of units may be used.

After the building heat transfer coefficients $U(I, J)$ have been input, the program finds the triangular factors of the symmetric heat transfer *matrix*, and uses them to solve the linear equations for the temperature variables (see Appendix A). It does this for one or more sets of heat source/climate data. As explained in the main text, ZONESTEAD is particularly useful for predicting performance of a building averaged over some time period. It gives results many times faster than the times needed to compute detailed temperature variations.

Building Data

Building data are input starting at line 200 as follows:

1. *Title.* A title is input, indicating the building being simulated, with names and node numbers of each building zone.
2. *Number of variable and fixed nodes (M, F).* There are M variable nodes, representing zones in which temperature varies and heat sources are specified, and F fixed nodes, including the ambient and any interior nodes in which temperature is kept constant.
3. *Heat transfer coefficients (U(I, J)).* Arcs of the network are represented by a two-dimensional array of heat transfer coefficients $U(I, J)$ between nodes I and J. For example, the coefficient between zones 1 and 4 is $U(1, 4)$. The coefficient is the sum of the thermal transmittances for all the common boundaries between the two zones. They must be input in this order: $U(1, 2)$, $U(1, 3), \ldots, U(1, N)$, then $U(2, 3), \ldots, U(M, N)$. Note that it is not necessary to enter coefficients between fixed nodes.

The method for finding the thermal transmittance for composite walls is given in the "Thermal Insulation" section in chapter 2. Surface transmittance and the component of the transfer coefficient due to infiltration (U_{inf}) are found by the conventional methods outlined in chapter 8. The procedure for determining transmittance due to natural convection or use of fans is presented in chapter 11.

Climate Data

Several sets of heat source/climate data can now be input, corresponding to climatic conditions for different days, average values for different months, and so forth. These are the constant inputs for each node. Each set consists of:

1. *Heat sources (Q(I), I = 1 to M)*. The solar gain to each zone is obtained by multiplying the monthly average gain by the appropriate area of glass exposed. Tables of monthly average radiation values are given in the appendices for equator-facing horizontal and vertical surfaces in different locations around the world. The computer program SOLRAD computes solar radiation for surfaces with any inclination or orientation in any location, for any sequence of days, using numbers of bright sunshine hours as data. In either case, the solar gain must be multiplied by the transmissivity of the glazing. A typical value for double glazing is 0.8. Internal gain is added to solar gain for living areas.
2. *Fixed temperatures (T(M + 1) to T(N))*. The specified temperatures of ambient and any other fixed node are input on the same line as the heat sources.

After the last climate data set, enter "END" to end the run.

Note. See the ZONESTEAD computer program listing on p. 89 in the appendix at the end of this chapter.

Example

The steady-state simulation of the Saunders' solar sandwich, given in chapter 9, is elaborated here.

Building Data

Title, number of nodes
```
200   DATA "ZONESTEAD: SOLAR SANDWICH—ZONES: ATTIC (1–2);
         INTERIOR (3); SUNSPACE (4); ROCKBED (5); AMBIENT (6)
201   DATA 5,1
```

Following the program title, line 201 gives the number of variable and fixed nodes. In this example, nodes 1–5 are variable and the ambient, node 6, is fixed.

Heat transfer coefficients
```
202   DATA 50,0,5,0,5
203   DATA 20,2,0,0
204   DATA 30,40,25
205   DATA 0,100
206   DATA 15
```

Lines 202–206 give the transfer matrix array, where the conductances between each zone are given (in W/°C). In line 203, for example, the transmittance between the bottom layer of the attic (zone 2) and the interior (zone 3) is 20 W/°C. This figure is obtained by multiplying the total area (m²) between these zones by the transmittance value (W/m² × °C) for the particular building material used. The two zeros at the end of line 203 indicate that no part of the bottom attic is exposed to the rockbed (5) or ambient (6).

Climate Data

207 DATA "NOV", 595,100,1050,445,0,2
208 DATA "DEC", 720,120,1060,540,0,−8
209 DATA "JAN", 900,150,1075,675,0,−11
210 DATA "FEB", 1215,200,1100,1815,0,−8,"END"

Each line gives a subtitle, followed by the gains for each of nodes 1–5, and temperature for node 6. A uniform internal gain of 1,000 W is added to any solar gain in node 3, the interior. Node 5, the rockbed, has no direct gain. The final figure in each line is the average ambient temperature for that month.

Output

ZONESTEAD prints out as follows:

ZONESTEAD: SOLAR SANDWICH − ZONES: ATTIC (1−2);
        INTERIOR (3); SUNSPACE (4); ROCKBED (5); AMBIENT (6)

HEAT TRANSFER COEFFTS
        50   0   5   0   5
             20   2   0   0
                  30 40   25
                       0 100
                          15

| TITLE | \multicolumn{6}{c}{DATA} | | | | | | \multicolumn{6}{c}{RESULTS} | | | | | |

| TITLE | \multicolumn{4}{c}{SOURCES} | | | TEMP | | | TEMP | | | \multicolumn{3}{c}{HEAT FLOW} | | |

	1	2	3	4	5	6	ZONES	1	2	3	4	5	6
NOV	595	100	1050	445	0	2		45	40	27	13	20	2190
DEC	720	120	1060	540	0	−8		42	36	19	4	12	2440
JAN	900	150	1075	675	0	−11		49	41	19	3	11	2800
FEB	1215	200	1100	1815	0	−8		73	62	30	18	20	4330

The results show that the average interior temperature is sufficient to maintain comfort for the whole winter. The temperatures in November and February are so high that ventilation with fans would be required for those months. However, they do not indicate whether or not temperature fluctuations would necessitate use of auxiliary heat during cold spells or ventilation during mild spells. A temperature-varying simulation with NETSPEC is needed for this.

NETSPEC

This BASIC program uses the modal method to compute temperature and heat flow variations in a thermal network with the same specifications as in ZONESTEAD, except that now it is also necessary to specify the thermal masses $C(I)$ of each node, as well as the internode heat transfer coefficients $U(I,J)$. Any consistent set of units may be used.

After the building data have been input for one or more "states," the program computes and prints the modal time constants and computes the modal eigenvectors for each mode. It then computes and prints the temperatures in each node at the end of each interval in a simulated weather cycle, with building data corresponding to a particular state for each interval.

NETSPEC is the most general of the three fundamental programs presented, but also the longest program, with the longest running time.

Building Data

1. *Title, number of variable and fixed nodes (M, F).* Same as ZONESTEAD.
2. *Thermal masses (C(I); I = 1 to M).* The thermal masses in the variable nodes are input.
3. *Number of states (S).* It is possible to use different heat transfer coefficients for different intervals in the run, corresponding to the addition of movable insulation, use of a fan, and so forth. Each configuration is called a state.
4. *Heat transfer coefficients U(I, J).* These are input in the same manner as in ZONESTEAD, but with a new set of coefficients for each state.

Input
DATA are entered as DATA statements starting at line 200:

Building Title
M, F
C(1), *C*(2) . . . *C*(*M*), *S*
U(1,2), *U*(1,3), . . . , *U*(1,*N*), *U*(2,3), . . . , *U*(*M*,*N*) for each state in
turn, *L* = 1 to *S*.

Climate Data

The building data are followed by one or more sets of climate data, each set consisting of

1. *Subtitle, initial temperatures (T(I); I = 1 to M).* A problem unique to NETSPEC is the choice of initial temperatures. One simple solution is to use average temperatures computed by ZONESTEAD for the same network. Another is to iterate the initial conditions until a cycle is obtained. To do this, an educated guess is made for initial temperatures and the program is run. The temperatures at the end of the cycle are now used as initial temperatures, and so on, until final and initial conditions are the same. This can be done quite quickly for a long cycle, where final conditions are not strongly dependent on initial conditions, but otherwise may be time consuming.
2. *Number of intervals (NI).* Each cycle to be simulated is split up into a number of intervals corresponding to periods with differing climatic input, and possibly different states. For each interval, there is the following information:
   (a) *Time duration (HRS).* The intervals can be unequal in length and often correspond to day and night conditions for a series of days, but shorter time steps can be used.
   (b) *State (L).* The number of the state, according to the order that the states were input.
   (c) *Heat source/climate data (Q(I), I = 1 to M; T(I), I = M + 1 to N).* Heat sources and fixed temperatures are input as in ZONESTEAD.

Input

For each set of climate data, input: subtitle, initial temperatures, number of intervals.

For each interval:

HRS, L, $Q(1)$, $Q(2)$, . . . , $Q(M)$, $T(M+1)$, . . . , $T(N)$.

After last climate data set, enter "END" to end the run. Data and results are printed either to the video screen, or to the printer.

Note. See the NETSPEC computer program listing on p. 90 in the appendix at the end of this chapter.

Example 1

This example uses the Saunders' solar sandwich building data given in the section on ZONESTEAD and examines the variations in the network as three different heat transfer states are employed. These states simulate the forced transfer of heat by a variable speed fan from the bottom layer of the attic to the rockbed. In state 0 the fan is off and in state 2 it is at full speed.

Building Data

```
200   DATA "SOLAR SANDWICH DESIGN—ZONES: ATTIC (1–2);
               INTERIOR (3); SUNSPACE (4); ROCKS (5); AMBIENT (6)
201   DATA 5,1
202   DATA 2000,1000,1000,1000,1000,3
203   DATA 50,0,5,0,5,20,2,0,0,30,40,25,0,100,15
204   DATA 50,0,5,10,5,20,2,0,0,30,40,25,0,100,15
205   DATA 50,0,5,20,5,20,2,0,0,30,40,25,0,100,15
```

The building data entry is similar to that of ZONESTEAD, but in line 202 the thermal masses of each zone are entered in Whr/°C, then the number of states, which in this case is 3. The transfer coefficients are obtained in the same manner as those used in ZONESTEAD. In lines 203, 204, and 205 the fourth number is the thermal transmittance from node 1 to node 5, which is 0 normally, but can be increased to 10 or 20 by turning on a fan.

Climate Data

```
206   DATA "4 DAY CYCLE—WITH FAN", 27,27,20,2,17
207   DATA 8
208   DATA 8,0,6000,1000,1500,4500,0,0
209   DATA 16,0,0,0,1000,0,0,−6
210   DATA 8,0,600,100,1050,450,0,0
211   DATA 16,1,0,0,1000,0,0,−6
212   DATA 8,1,600,100,1050,450,0,0
213   DATA 16,1,0,0,1000,0,0,−6
214   DATA 8,1,600,100,1050,450,0,0
215   DATA 16,2,0,0,1000,0,0,−6,"END"
```

Line 206 gives the cycle title, followed by the initial temperatures in each of the zones. As mentioned previously, the fastest way to obtain these initial temperatures is to run the data through the ZONESTEAD program, using line 203 for the transfer matrix. Line 207 gives the number of intervals, in this case, 4 days and 4 nights.

Line 208 gives the data for the first day. It is 8 hr long and the fan is off, state 0. There is a 6,000, 1,000, 500, and 4,500 W solar gain to zones 1, 2, 3, and 4, respectively. In addition, zone 3 has 1,000 W of internal gain. The rockbed receives no direct gain and the ambient temperature, zone 6, is 0°C.

The data for the remaining days and nights follows the pattern used in ZONESTEAD. However, as the cycle progresses the fan speed is increased, so that by the last interval the fan is at full speed, state 2.

Output

NETSPEC prints out as follows:

NETSPEC: SOLAR SANDWICH DESIGN: ZONES: ATTIC (1–2); INTERIOR (3);
SUNSPACE (4); ROCKS (5); AMBIENT (6)
THERMAL MASSES: 2000   1000   1000   1000   1000

STATE 0 TRANSFER COEFFTS

```
      50    0    5    0    5
           20    2    0    0
                30   40   25
                      0  100
                          15
```

TIME CONSTANTS: 127   30   11   9   6

STATE 1 TRANSFER COEFFTS

```
      50    0    5   10    5
           20    2    0    0
                30   40   25
                      0  100
                          15
```

TIME CONSTANTS: 108   23   11   9   6

STATE 2 TRANSFER COEFFTS

```
      50    0    5   20    5
           20    2    0    0
                30   40   25
                      0  100
                          15
```

TIME CONSTANTS: 101   18   11   9   6

4-DAY CYCLE; WITH FAN

HR	STATE	GAIN (W) DATA					°C	RESULTS °C				
	NODE: 1	2	3	4	5	6	1	2	3	4	5
0								27	27	20	2	17
8	0	6000	1000	1500	4500	0	0	48	36	26	27	17
24	0	0	0	1000	0	0	−6	42	37	23	6	16
32	0	600	100	1050	450	0	0	42	37	23	9	17
48	1	0	0	1000	0	0	−6	36	34	21	3	17
56	1	600	100	1050	450	0	0	36	33	22	8	18
72	1	0	0	1000	0	0	−6	31	30	20	2	17
80	1	600	100	1050	450	0	0	32	30	21	7	17
96	2	0	0	1000	0	0	−6	27	27	20	2	17

TOTAL KWhr   221

The printout for a run with the same climate data, but no fan (state 0 through-out) is now given. The temperatures are higher in the attic and lower in the rock store.

4-DAY CYCLE; NO FAN

HR	STATE	GAIN (W) DATA					°C	RESULTS °C				
	NODE: 1	2	3	4	5	6	1	2	3	4	5
0								33	31	19	2	13
8	0	6000	1000	1500	4500	0	0	54	40	25	27	14
24	0	0	0	1000	0	0	−6	47	41	23	6	15
32	0	600	100	1050	450	0	0	46	41	23	9	16
48	0	0	0	1000	0	0	−6	41	37	21	3	15
56	0	600	100	1050	450	0	0	41	37	22	8	15
72	0	0	0	1000	0	0	−6	37	34	20	3	14
80	0	600	100	1050	450	0	0	37	33	21	7	14
96	0	0	0	1000	0	0	−6	33	31	19	2	13
TOTAL KWhr							221					

Example 2

The NETSPEC printout for the hot climate solar wall, explained in chapter 10, is given here. This example demonstrates the principles of passive solar cooling.

WALL (1–3); INTERIOR (4); AMBIENT (5)
THERMAL MASSES: 2500   2500   2500   1000

STATE 0 TRANSFER COEFFTS
```
      450      0      0   425
             450      0     0
                    280     0
                          160
```

TIME CONSTANTS: 19.8   3.9   2   1.6

STATE 1 TRANSFER COEFFTS
```
      450      0      0   425
             450      0     0
                    280     0
                          800
```

TIME CONSTANTS: 13.9   3.3   1.7   .9

WINTER MILD 1-DAY CYCLE

TIME	STATE	SOURCES					TEMP/RESULTS TEMPS			
	NODE: 1	2	3	4	5		1	2	3	4
0							14	20	22	19
8	0	30000	0	0	3000	10	52	34	27	26
24	0	0	0	0	1200	5	14	20	22	19

SUMMER HOT 1-DAY CYCLE, WITH VENT OPEN AT NIGHT

TIME	STATE	SOURCES					TEMP/RESULTS TEMPS			
	NODE: 1	2	3	4	5		1	2	3	4
0							22	24	24	20
4	0	0	0	0	300	24	23	23	23	24
12	0	4000	0	0	300	30	32	28	26	28
16	1	0	0	0	300	24	27	28	27	25
24	1	0	0	0	300	18	22	24	24	20

WALLSPEC

This BASIC program uses the modal method to compute temperature variations through a homogeneous wall that is coupled to a single interior space node and to the specified ambient temperature. The interior space node represents the thermal properties of the rest of the building.

The main use of WALLSPEC is for simulating the temperature variations in a Trombe wall, when the solar gain goes into the outside wall surface heat source ($Q0$); or in a direct gain system with thermal storage in a thick wall, when the solar gain is divided between the interior wall surface ($Q1$) and the interior space node ($Q2$).

WALLSPEC requires no initial conditions to be specified. It assumes cyclic temperature and heat source conditions in which the final state after NI intervals is the same as the initial state. Any consistent set of units may be used.

Building Data

1. *Variable subscripts.* Thermal mass (C) and thermal transmittance (U) are followed by a subscript indicating the part of the wall or interior node with which they are associated.

   C and U, without subscript, denote thermal mass and transmittance of the wall, subscript 0 denotes outer surface of the wall, subscript 1 denotes inner surface of the wall, subscript 2 denotes interior space.
2. *Thermal mass.* C is the thermal mass of the wall; $C2$ is the thermal mass in the interior of the house.
3. *Thermal transmittances.* Unlike the network approach, surface thermal transmittances are considered separately from wall transmittances. They are calculated by the conventional methods outlined in chapter 8.

   U is the thermal transmittance of the wall; $U0$ is thermal transmittance from outer wall surface to ambient; $U1$ is thermal transmittance from inner wall surface to interior; $U2$ is thermal transmittance from interior to ambient other than through the wall, that is, through all the other exterior walls, windows, and roof.
4. *Number of modes (M).* The user may specify the number of modes to be used; the program prints out the time constants for the specified number. Normally, not more than three modes are needed, unless variations over very short transient times are required. The user may then experiment with different numbers of modes.

Input

DATA are entered as DATA statements starting at line 200, first a building title followed by building data in order:

Title, C, $C2$, U, $U0$, $U1$, $U2$, M.

Climate Data

The building data are followed by one or more sets of climate data. Each set consists of

1. *Subtitle*
2. *Number of intervals (NI).* Each cycle to be simulated is split up into a number of intervals corresponding to periods with differing climatic input. For each interval there is the following information:
   (a) *Time duration (HRS).* The intervals can be unequal in length and often correspond to day and night conditions for a series of days, but shorter time steps can be used.
   (b) *Heat sources.* $Q0$ is the solar gain on the outer surface of the wall. If the wall is glazed, the transmittance of the glazing must be taken into account. $Q1$ is the solar gain to the interior surface(s) of the wall, coming from windows in other walls. $Q2$ is the solar gain to the thermal mass materials in the interior of the house added to the internal gain.
   (c) *Ambient temperature (A).* Constant for an interval.

Input

For each climate set, enter data in order: Subtitle, *NI*.
For each interval:

HRS, *Q0, Q1, Q2, A.*

After last climate data set, enter "END" to end the run.

Note. See the WALLSPEC computer program listing on p. 94 in the appendix at the end of this chapter.

Example 1

A Trombe wall 50 m² in area and 30 cm thick, introduced in chapter 10, is examined in detail.

Building Data

```
200   DATA "TROMBE WALL: 50 SQM OF 30 CM THICK WALL"
201   DATA 7500,1500,150,125,500,85,3
```

The title is given and then the thermal mass, in Whr/°C, of the wall and interior space. The transmittances follow: that of the total wall is 150, of the outer wall surface 125, of the inner wall surface 500, and of the interior space 85. Three modes are used in this example.

Climate Data

```
202   DATA "3 DAY CYCLE", 6
203   DATA 8, 30000,0,1000,0
204   DATA 16,0,0,1000,-6
205   DATA 8,3000,0,1000,0
206   DATA 16,0,0,1000,-6
207   DATA 8,3000,0,1000,0
208   DATA 16,0,0,1000,-6,"END"
```

The cycle title is given in line 202 followed by the number of intervals. In this example, six intervals are used, three days and three nights.

Line 203 gives the data for the first day. It is an 8-hr interval and the gain on the outer surface of the wall is 30,000 W. The interior wall surface receives no gain and the interior space has a steady internal gain of 1,000 W. The ambient temperature is 0°C.

The night is 16 hr in duration and there is no gain to either surface of the wall, but the 1,000 W gain to the interior remains. The ambient temperature is −6°C.

The second and third days are similar, but the gain to the outer wall surface is reduced to 3,000 W (10% of the first day) to simulate a cloudy period.

Output

WALLSPEC prints out the following results:

TROMBE WALL: 50 SQM of 30 CM THICK WALL
WALL: THERMAL MASS 7500; CONDUCTANCE 150
      OUTER & INNER SURFACE CONDUCTANCES 125 500
SPACE: THERMAL MASS 1500; CONDUCTANCE 85
4 TIME CONSTANTS: 49.3 6 2.3 1

3 DAY CYCLE

| TIME | SOURCES | | | AMB | TEMPS | | |
	OUT (WALL)	IN	SPACE	TEMP	OUT (WALL)	IN	SPACE
8	30000	0	1000	0	77	15	13
16	0	0	1000	−6	18	22	20
8	3000	0	1000	0	22	21	20
16	0	0	1000	−6	11	16	16
8	3000	0	1000	0	17	15	15
16	0	0	1000	−6	7	12	12

Although time constants are given for each node, only the first one supplies a useful indication of the heat-storage capabilities of the wall. Note that after the approximately 48-hr time constant, internal temperature falls substantially. This example demonstrates the inability of the Trombe wall to store heat for even a short cloudy period with relatively mild winter temperatures.

Example 2

The direct gain design with solar wall is discussed in chapter 10, with results in Table 10.1.

Note. See the Direct gain–Solar Wall computer program printout on p. 96 in the appendix at the end of this chapter.

SUNSPEC

This microcomputer interactive simulation package program simulates the annual thermal behavior of a zoned energy-efficient building with significant passive solar gain using a linear network model of the building. The simplified simulation procedures described in chapter 11 are incorporated, together with the NETSPEC calculation of temperature variations and heat flows.

The program is interactive, with prompts to the user to provide necessary building and weather data. On completion of a computer run, the current data may be filed on tape or disk, so the first question on starting a new run is whether the data are to be input from the keyboard or from a previously stored file. When entering data from the keyboard, the user inputs the number of zones and then area, thermal properties, internal heat gain and minimum comfort temperature for each zone, and simple climatological data.

The building can be divided into up to four zones. Within the computer program, the building is represented by a network with one node for each zone plus two extra nodes to represent the building foundation plus the building structure adjacent to the main living zone. The program user is required to input data for each zone; for the floor, wall, roof, and ground areas and corresponding insulation levels; an estimate of the thermal mass on a scale of 1 to 4; and the air infiltration in air changes per hour. Areas of windows with different orientations are input with number of panes, and the insulation values of any night insulation used. Between each pair of zones, total transmittance (area/RSI) must be input.

Simple climatological data required include the design temperature, number of months in the heating season (that is, with over 100 degree days Celsius), the total heating degree days, and the number of bright sunshine hours. For each zone, the average solar shading, internal gain, and required comfort temperature are input.

The temperature of the main living zone (entered last) is maintained strictly at or above the specified comfort level, by adding auxiliary heat as necessary. Temperature setback may be specified for 6 night hours and/or 8 day hours. After setback, a 2-hr recovery period is allowed to restore the zone temperature to the normal comfort level. For all other zones the comfort level is maintained only approximately, but usually within 1°C.

The computer program uses the simplified climatological data to compute the temperature variations on three typical days. A mild, sunny day enables an assessment of possible solar overheating; a cold, sunless day with temperature dropping to the design temperature gives the peak auxiliary heating required; an average winter day fills in the information needed to assess the annual heating load. Each day is divided into five time intervals, including a 6-hr night period, a 2-hr early morning period (for temperature recovery if the night temperature has been set back), an 8-hr day period, a 2-hr early evening period (for temperature recovery after day setback), and a 6-hr evening period.

The program was developed simultaneously on two extremely different microcomputers, an inexpensive Commodore VIC 20, with only 11K RAM and cassette file storage, and an IBM personal computer with hard disk drive. A complete two-zone run takes 2 min on the VIC and rather less on the IBM. When the program is run from disk, the disk also contains an information program, SUNINFO, which gives full information about running SUNSPEC. SUNINFO is described in the next section.

The Program SUNINFO — Information About SUNSPEC

Follow the prompts provided. At the first prompt: K(EY) or FILENAME? Type K to enter data from the keyboard, or type the filename if you have previously stored a data file.

Be ready to input the building, climate, and temperature metric data. Wall area is all above-ground wall area. Ground area is area of all below-ground walls and floors.

The RSI for concrete footings and ground floors is normally about 0.2, plus the RSI of any insulation installed. The night RSI of any window insulation is 0.2 for a well-sealed extra air space, plus the insulation RSI. For the second and higher zones, enter the heat conductance with all lower zones, in the form boundary area/RSI. The RSI of uninsulated interior partitions is approximately 0.5.

Any false entries can be corrected after each input page.

At the prompt, LINE#CHANGE OR N(EXT), type N if ready to proceed, or type number of line to be changed. At the end of a run, the daily temperature variations and heat loads are displayed for the last zone. Type the zone number for display of another zone.

For a repeat calculation with changed data, type:

> S for new setback data,
> T for new temperature and climate data,
> Z for new building zone data.

Type E to end the run, or type the filename to file current data for later reuse.

The program runs in two stages, with a slight pause between. The building data are used to compute modal parameters, which are then used with the climate/temperature data to calculate daily temperature variations and heatloads. To speed up program operation, note the following:

1. If possible, repeat simulations with different climate/temperature data for the same building data. Changing the building data takes extra time.
2. Although you may divide the building into up to four temperature zones, program running time increases with the number of zones. If possible, use only one or two zones in the early stages of a design study.

Note. See the SUNSPEC computer program listing printout on p. 97 in the appendix at the end of this chapter.

A Typical Interactive Computer Run with SUNSPEC: Temperatures and Heatloads in a Zoned Passive Solar Building

This simulation is for a well-sealed and insulated one-and-a-half storey home with full basement. The basement and first storey each have floor area of 100 m^2; the second storey has floor area 40 m^2. The basement is taken as zone 1; the first and second storeys together are the main living area, zone 2. The weather data are typical for central Canada. Significant passive solar gain in zone 2 on a sunny day causes the temperature to rise to 27°C.

Note. See the SUNSPEC interactive run printout on p. 103 in the appendix at the end of this chapter.

Conclusions

The building modeled with night setback requires peak auxiliary heat of 10.6 kW in the main living zone, 2.2 kW in the basement zone, and has a seasonal auxiliary heat requirement of 10,300 kWhr. Without using setback, the peak heat required in the main living zone is 4.6 kW, and the seasonal heat load is 10,960 kWhr. Thus the annual savings from night setback is only 600 kWhr in this energy-efficient building, and the peak heat required is more than doubled.

SOLRAD

SOLRAD is a computer program to be used in conjunction with all other programs and calculations in which a knowledge of solar gain is needed. It computes the average daily solar gain during any sequence of days in the calendar on a surface inclined or oriented in any direction, situated at any subarctic latitude. As such it is more versatile than climatological tables, particularly for inclined surfaces and those oriented away from the equator. It does require some estimate of the proportion of time the sun is out.

SOLRAD is interactive. It first prompts the user for latitude and interval of days, then computes the day length for that interval and prompts the user for the mean sunshine hours during the day. It then asks for ground *albedo* (see the Glossary) in order to compute ground-reflected radiation. The user then inputs the slope (in degrees from horizontal) and aspect (degrees from south, in the northern hemisphere) of the surface.

The program now prints out the beam (or direct), diffuse, and reflected solar radiation in Whr per m^2 of surface per day. It also totals these values.

A sample interactive run of SOLRAD is included in this chapter, as well as a computer listing of SOLRAD. The mathematics of this program are briefly explained in Appendix C.

Note. See the SOLRAD computer program listing on p. 105 in the appendix at the end of this chapter and the SOLRAD typical interactive run on p. 107.

APPENDIX

```
0  '  ***************************************************
1  '  *          ZONESTEAD: IBM PC: JULY 1986          *
2  '  *    STEADY STATE SOLUTION OF THERMAL NETWORK    *
3  '  *  M ZONES, GIVEN SOURCES; F ZONES, GIVEN TEMPS  *
4  '  ***************************************************
7  DIM A(9,7),D(7),Q(7),T(9)
9  '
10 ' 11-3 READ/PRINT TITLE, M,F. INITIALISE
11 READ T$,M,F:PRINT T$:P=M+1:N=M+F
12 FOR I=1 TO M:D(I)=0:NEXT
13 Z=5:W$="     ":S$=W$:FOR J=0 TO 3:S$=S$+S$:NEXT
19 '
21 PRINT:PRINT "TRANSFER COEFFTS
22 FOR I=1 TO M:P$="":X=Z*I
23 FOR J=I+1 TO N:READ A:GOSUB 91
24 IF J<P THEN D(J)=D(J)+A:A(I,J)=-A
25 A(J,I)=A:D(I)=D(I)+A:NEXT
26 PRINT P$:NEXT I:PRINT
29 '
30 ' 31-4 TRIANGULAR FACTORS OF TRANSFER MATRIX
31 FOR K=2 TO M
32 FOR I=1 TO K-1:A=A(I,K):C=A/D(I):D(K)=D(K)-C*A
33 FOR J=K+1 TO M:A(K,J)=A(K,J)-C*A(I,J):NEXT
34 NEXT I:NEXT K
39 '
40 ' 41 PRINT HEADINGS
41 P$="ZONES":X=Z:FOR A=1 TO N:GOSUB 91:NEXT:PRINT P$:X=Z
49 '
50 ' 51-4 READ/PRINT SUBTITLE. DATA SOURCES & TEMPS
51 READ U$:PRINT:IF U$="END" THEN 98
52 PRINT U$:P$="DATA: SOURCES ":GOSUB 94:PRINT P$" TEMPS
53 X=Z:P$="":FOR I=1 TO M:READ A:Q(I)=A:GOSUB 91:NEXT
54 FOR J=P TO N:READ A:T(J)=A:GOSUB 91:NEXT:PRINT P$
59 '
60 ' 61-7 COMPUTE T(I), Q(J)
61 FOR I=1 TO M:T=Q(I)
62 FOR J=P TO N:T=T+A(J,I)*T(J):NEXT
63 IF I>1 THEN FOR J=1 TO I-1:T=T-A(J,I)*T(J):NEXT
64 T(I)=T/D(I):NEXT I
65 FOR I=M-1 TO 1 STEP -1:T=0
66 FOR J=I+1 TO M:T=T+A(I,J)*T(J):NEXT
67 T(I)=T(I)-T/D(I):NEXT I
69 '
70 ' 71-5 PRINT T(I), Q(J)
71 P$="RESULTS:TEMPS ":GOSUB 94:PRINT P$" HEATFLOWS
72 X=Z:P$="":FOR I=1 TO M:A=T(I):GOSUB 91:NEXT
73 FOR J=P TO N:A=0
74 FOR I=1 TO M:A=A+A(J,I)*(T(I)-T(J)):NEXT
75 GOSUB 91:NEXT J:PRINT P$:GOTO 51
79 '
90 ' SUB 91: FORMATTED PRINT OF DATA & RESULTS
91 P$=P$+LEFT$(S$,X-LEN(P$))+STR$(INT(A+.5)):X=X+Z:RETURN
92 '
93 ' SUB 94 FORMATTED PRINT SPACING
94 IF M>2 THEN FOR I=3 TO M:P$=P$+W$:NEXT
95 RETURN
98 END
```

```
0  '  **********************************************************
1  ' *              NETSPEC: IBM PC: JULY 1986              *
2  ' *      TEMPERATURE VARIATIONS IN A THERMAL NETWORK      *
3  ' *    M NODES, GIVEN SOURCES;  F NODES, GIVEN TEMPS     *
4  '  **********************************************************
7  DIM A(7,7),B(7),C(7),D(7),E(7),G(4,8,7)
8  DIM Q(7),R(7),S(7),T(8),U(7),V(4,7,7)
9  '
10 ' READ/PRINT TITLE, M, F, INITIALISE
11 READ T$,M,F:PRINT T$:P=M+1:N=M+F:Y=1E-08:Z=6
12 W$="      ":S$=W$:FOR J=0 TO 3:S$=S$+S$:NEXT
19 '
20 ' READ/PRINT THERMAL MASSES
21 PRINT"THERMAL MASSES:":
22 FOR I=1 TO M:READ A:PRINT A::C(I)=A:R(I)=SQR(A):NEXT
23 PRINT
29 '
30 ' FOR S STATES READ/PRINT COEFFTS: FIND EIGENMODES
31 READ S:FOR L=0 TO S-1:PRINT "STATE"L"TRANSFER COEFFTS
32 FOR I=1 TO M:D(I)=0:NEXT
33 FOR I=1 TO M:P$="":X=Z*I
34 FOR J=I+1 TO N:READ A:GOSUB 91:G(L,J,I)=A
35 IF J<P THEN D(J)=D(J)+A:A(I,J)=-A/R(I)/R(J)
36 D(I)=D(I)+A:NEXT:PRINT P$
37 T(I)=D(I)/C(I):A(I,I)=T(I):NEXT I
38 PRINT "  TIME CONSTANTS:"::GOSUB 102:PRINT:NEXT L
39 '
40 ' READ/PRINT SUBTITLE: PRINT HEADINGS
41 PRINT:READ U$:IF U$="END" THEN END
42 PRINT U$:P$="TIME   STATE   SOURCES
43 IF M>1 THEN FOR I=2 TO M:P$=P$+W$:NEXT
44 P$=P$+"   TEMP
45 IF N>P THEN FOR J=P+1 TO N:P$=P$+W$:NEXT
46 PRINT P$"   RESULTS TEMPS":X=Z+Z:P$="    NODE:
47 FOR A=1 TO N:GOSUB 91:NEXT
48 FOR A=1 TO M:GOSUB 91:NEXT:PRINT P$
49 '                    NETSPEC - CONTD
```

```
49 '                    NETSPEC - CONTD
50 ' 51-2 INITIALISE: READ/PRINT INITIAL TEMPERATURES
51 P$=STR$(0):X=X-M*Z:S=0:FOR J=P TO N:U(J)=0:NEXT
52 FOR I=1 TO M:READ A:T(I)=A:GOSUB 91:NEXT:PRINT P$
59 '
60 ' 61-4 READ/PRINT DATA: INTERVAL,STATE,SOURCES,TEMPS
61 READ NI:FOR IN=1 TO NI:READ H
62 P$="":X=0:S=S+H:A=S:GOSUB 91:READ A:L=A:GOSUB 91
63 FOR I=1 TO M:READ A:Q(I)=A:GOSUB 91:NEXT
64 FOR J=P TO N:READ A:T(J)=A:GOSUB 91:NEXT
69 '
70 ' FIND TEMPS,T(I), & HEATFLOWS,Q(J)
71 FOR I=1 TO M:S(I)=C(I)*T(I)
72 FOR J=P TO N:Q(I)=Q(I)+G(L,J,I)*T(J):NEXT:NEXT I
73 FOR K=1 TO M:T=V(L,O,K):D=H*T:E=EXP(-D):F=(1-E)/D:A=0
74 B=0:FOR I=1 TO M:U=V(L,I,K):A=A+U*S(I):B=B+U*Q(I):NEXT
75 B=B/T:A=A-B:B(K)=A*E+B:R(K)=A*F+B:NEXT K
76 FOR I=1 TO M:A=0:B=0
77 FOR K=1 TO M:U=V(L,I,K):A=A+U*B(K):B=B+U*R(K):NEXT
78 T(I)=A:GOSUB 91
79 FOR J=P TO N:U(J)=U(J)+G(L,J,I)*(B-T(J))*H:NEXT
80 NEXT I:PRINT P$
81 NEXT IN:P$="TOTAL HEAT FLOWS/1000":X=P*Z+Z
82 FOR I=P TO N:A=U(I)/1000:GOSUB 91:NEXT:PRINT P$:GOTO 41
89 '
90 ' SUB 91: FORMATTED PRINT OF DATA/RESULTS
91 P$=P$+LEFT$(S$,X-LEN(P$))+STR$(INT(A+.5)):X=X+Z:RETURN
99 '                    NETSPEC - CONTD
```

```
 99 '                     NETSPEC - CONTD
100 ' SUB 102  FIND EIGENMODES
101 ' 102-112 HOUSEHOLDER TRIDIAGONALISATION
102 FOR K=2 TO M:O=K-1:G=A(O,K):E=G*G:H=O:IF K=M THEN 112
103 B(K)=0:FOR J=K+1 TO M:A=A(O,J):H=H+A*A:B(J)=0:NEXT
104 E=E+H:D=0:IF H=0 THEN 112
105 B=G:G=-SGN(G+Y)*SQR(E):A(O,K)=B-G:H=E-B*G
106 FOR I=K TO M:C=A(O,I):B=B(I)+A(I,I)*C:IF I=M THEN 108
107 FOR J=I+1 TO M:A=A(I,J):B=B+A*A(O,J):B(J)=B(J)+A*C:NEXT
108 B(I)=B:D=D+B*C:NEXT I:D=D/2/H/H
109 FOR J=K TO M:C=A(O,J):B=B(J)/H-D*C:B(J)=B
110 ' SYMMETRIC TRIDIAGONAL FACTORS IN ARRAYS T & E
111 FOR I=K TO J:A(I,J)=A(I,J)-A(O,I)*B-C*B(I):NEXT:NEXT J
112 S(O)=H:B(O)=G:E(O)=E/T(O):T(K)=A(K,K)-E(O):NEXT K
119 '
120 ' M UNSHIFTED LR STEPS, THEN SHIFT & RESTORE
121 R=M:T=0:FOR J=1 TO M:GOSUB 161:NEXT
122 FOR R=M TO 2 STEP -1
123 T=T(R):GOSUB 161:T=-T:GOSUB 161
124 IF ABS(E(R-1))>Y THEN 123
125 NEXT R
129 '
130 ' EIGENVALUES IN INCREASING ORDER
131 J=M:FOR K=M TO R+1 STEP -1:O=K-1:T=T(K)
132 IF T<T(O) THEN T(K)=T(O):T(O)=T:J=K
133 NEXT:R=J:IF J<M THEN 131
139 '
140 ' TRIDIAG. EIGENVECTORS BY INVERSE ITERATION
141 FOR R=1 TO M:T=T(R):PRINT INT(10/T+.5)/10;:E=0
142 FOR K=1 TO M:Q=A(K,K)-T-B(K-1)*E:IF ABS(Q)<Y THEN Q=Y
143 E=B(K)/Q:E(K)=E:Q(K)=Q:U(K)=1:NEXT
144 FOR K=2 TO M:U(K)=U(K)-E(K-1)*U(K-1):NEXT:E=0
145 FOR K=M TO 1 STEP -1:U=U(K)/Q(K)-E:E=E(K-1)*U:U(K)=U*Y
146 NEXT K
149 '
150 ' EIGENVALUES & NORMALISED VECTORS IN ARRAY V
151 FOR K=M-1 TO 2 STEP -1:O=K-1:H=S(O):IF H=0 THEN 154
152 D=0:FOR I=K TO M:D=D+A(O,I)*U(I):NEXT:D=D/H
153 FOR I=K TO M:U(I)=U(I)-D*A(O,I):NEXT
154 NEXT K:D=0:FOR I=1 TO M:D=D+U(I)^2:NEXT:D=SQR(D)
155 V(L,O,R)=T:FOR I=1 TO M:V(L,I,R)=U(I)/R(I)/D:NEXT
156 NEXT R:RETURN
159 '
160 ' SUB 161  LR RECURSION RELATION
161 E=T:FOR K=1 TO R-1:T(K)=T(K)+E(K)-E
162 E(K)=E(K)*T(K+1)/T(K):E=E(K)+T:NEXT
163 T(R)=T(R)-E:RETURN
```

A SAMPLE RUN OF NETSPEC

```
200 DATA"SOLAR SANDWICH:ATTIC(1,2):INTERIOR(3):SUNSPACE(4):ROCKS(5):AMB(6)
201 DATA 5,1
202 DATA 2000,1000,1000,1000,1000,3
203 DATA 50,0,5, 0,5,20,2,0,0,30,40,25,0,100,15
204 DATA 50,0,5,10,5,20,2,0,0,30,40,25,0,100,15
205 DATA 50,0,5,20,5,20,2,0,0,30,40,25,0,100,15
206 DATA "4 DAY CYCLE - WITH FAN",27,27,20,2,17
207 DATA 8
208 DATA 8,0,6000,1000,1500,4500,0,0
209 DATA 16,0,0,0,1000,0,0,-6
210 DATA 8,0,600,100,1050,450,0,0
211 DATA 16,1,0,0,1000,0,0,-6
212 DATA 8,1,600,100,1050,450,0,0
213 DATA 16,1,0,0,1000,0,0,-6
214 DATA 8,1,600,100,1050,450,0,0
215 DATA 16,2,0,0,1000,0,0,-6,"END"
```

```
SOLAR SANDWICH:ATTIC(1,2):INTERIOR(3):SUNSPACE(4):ROCKS(5):AMB(6)
THERMAL MASSES: 2000   1000   1000   1000   1000
STATE 0 TRANSFER COEFFTS
        50      0      5      0      5
               20      2      0      0
                      30     40     25
                              0    100
                                    15
    TIME CONSTANTS: 127   30.2   11.5   8.7   6
STATE 1 TRANSFER COEFFTS
        50      0      5     10      5
               20      2      0      0
                      30     40     25
                              0    100
                                    15
    TIME CONSTANTS: 108.5   22.8   11.5   8.5   6


STATE 2 TRANSFER COEFFTS
        50      0      5     20      5
               20      2      0      0
                      30     40     25
                              0    100
                                    15
    TIME CONSTANTS: 101.1   18.4   11.5   8.3   6
```

```
4 DAY CYCLE - WITH FAN
TIME  STATE  SOURCES                          TEMP  RESULTS TEMPS
      NODE:    1      2      3      4      5     6     1    2    3    4    5
 0                                                   27   27   20    2   17
 8      0    6000   1000   1500   4500    0    0    48   36   26   27   17
24      0      0      0    1000      0    0   -6    42   37   23    6   16
32      0     600    100   1050    450    0    0    42   37   23    9   17
48      1      0      0    1000      0    0   -6    36   34   21    3   17
56      1     600    100   1050    450    0    0    36   33   22    8   18
72      1      0      0    1000      0    0   -6    31   30   20    2   17
80      1     600    100   1050    450    0    0    32   30   21    7   17
96      2      0      0    1000      0    0   -6    27   27   20    2   17
TOTAL HEAT FLOWS/1000                             221
```

```
0  '  *************************************************************
1  ' *              WALLSPEC: IBM PC: JULY 1986                *
2  ' * TEMPERATURE VARIATIONS IN A WALL & ONE SPACE NODE       *
3  ' *   WALL(OUTER SURFACE, O: INNER, 1): SPACE NODE, 2       *
4  ' *************************************************************
7  DIM A(9),B(2,9),E(9,9),N(9),P$(9)
8  DIM P(9),Q(9),S(9,3),U(9,9),W(2,9)
9  '
10 '  11-5 READ/PRINT TITLE, THERMAL MASSES, CONDUCTANCES
11 READ T$:PRINT T$:S$="          ":Z=6
12 READ C,C2,U,UO,U1,U2
13 PRINT "WALL:THERMAL MASS"C": CONDUCTANCE"U
14 PRINT "     OUTER & INNER SURFACE CONDUCTANCES"UO:U1
15 PRINT "SPACE:THERMAL MASS"C2": CONDUCTANCE"U2
19 '
20 '  21-48 READ #MODES, M: FIND MODES, K=0 TO M-1
21 READ M:PRINT M"TIME CONSTANTS: ";:M=M-1
22 R=1/U:RO=1/UO+R:R2=1/U1+1/U2:H=C*R:C2=C2/C
23 XO=R*UO:X1=R*U1:YO=UO*RO:Y2=U2*R2:X2=1/Y2
24 W=C2*X2/X1:W1=1+W:DO=1.2/W1:D1=DO/2:D2=D1/2
25 KO=1+.4/SQR(W):X3=XO+X1:X4=XO*X1:X5=X1*X2
26 X=(X3-X5)/W1:A=SQR(X/(1+X/3)):PI=3.14159
27 FOR K=0 TO M:IF K THEN A=A+DO:GOTO 31
28 IF K>KO THEN A=K*PI-PI:A=A+X2/A
29 '
30 '  31-5 ITERATION ON EIGENVALUE, A
31 B=A*A:V=W*B:U=1-V:Y=B-X4:F=Y*U+X4*X2:G=(X3*U-X5)*A
32 C=COS(A):S=SIN(A):F1=2*A*(U-W*Y):G1=X3-X5-3*X3*V
33 D=(G*C-F*S)/((F-G1)*C+(G+F1)*S)
34 IF D>D1 OR D<-D2 THEN D=D1
35 A=A+D:IF ABS(D)>.000001 THEN 31
39 '
40 '  41-6 PRINT TIME CONSTANT: FIND EIGENFUNCTIONS
41 B=A*A:P=B/H:PRINT INT(10/P+.5)/10;:P(K)=P
42 F=ATN(XO/A):SO=SIN(F):S1=SIN(A-F)
43 CO=COS(F):C1=COS(A-F):X=(C1-CO)/A
44 V=X2*C1/(1-W*B):U=V*A*C2:D=(A+SO*CO+S1*C1)/2+V*U
45 B(O,K)=CO:B(1,K)=C1:B(2,K)=V
46 W(O,K)=(SO-X)/D:W(1,K)=(S1+X)/D:W(2,K)=U/D
47 '
48 NEXT K:PRINT
49 '              WALLSPEC - CONTD
```

A SAMPLE RUN OF WALLSPEC

```
49 '                WALLSPEC - CONTD
50 ' 52-3 READ/PRINT SUBTITLE.U$. #INTERVALS.N
51 ' 54-6 PRINT HEADINGS: INITIALISE
52 READ U$:IF U$="END" THEN 98
53 PRINT:PRINT U$:READ N
54 PRINT"TIME  SOURCES              AMB          TEMPS
55 PRINT"     OUT(WALL)IN  SPACE   TEMP       OUT(WALL)IN  SPACE
56 FOR K=0 TO M:A(K)=0:N(K)=1:NEXT
59 '
60 ' 61-3 READ/PRINT INTERVAL: SOURCES.Q0.Q1.Q2: AMB.TEMP
61 FOR I=1 TO N:X=0:P$="":READ A:H(I)=A:GOSUB 91
62 READ A:GOSUB 91:Q0=A:READ A:GOSUB 91:Q1=A
63 READ A:GOSUB 91:Q2=A:READ A:GOSUB 91:P$(I)=P$
65 ' 66-7 STEADY STATE TEMPS. S(I.J)
66 T1=(Q1+Q0/Y0+Q2/Y2)*R0*R2/(R0+R2):S(I.1)=T1+A
67 S(I.0)=(T1+Q0/U)/Y0+A:S(I.2)=(T1+Q2/U1)/Y2+A
69 '
70 ' 71-4 1ST CYCLE RUN TO FIND INITIAL A(K)
71 FOR K=0 TO M:E(I.K)=EXP(-H(I)*P(K)):NEXT
72 IF I>1 THEN GOSUB 94
73 NEXT I:I=1:FOR J=0 TO 2:S(0.J)=S(N.J):NEXT:GOSUB 94
74 FOR K=0 TO M:A(K)=A(K)/(1-N(K)):NEXT
79 '
80 ' 81-6 FOR EACH INTERVAL. FIND A(K). TEMPS: PRINT
81 FOR I=1 TO N:P$=P$(I):X=6*Z:IF I=1 THEN 83
82 FOR K=0 TO M:A(K)=(A(K)+U(I.K))*E(I.K):NEXT
83 FOR J=0 TO 2:A=S(I.J)
84 FOR K=0 TO M:A=A-B(J.K)*A(K):NEXT
85 GOSUB 91:NEXT J:PRINT P$
86 NEXT I:GOTO 51
89 '
90 ' SUB 91: FORMATTED PRINT OF DATA & RESULTS
91 P$=P$+LEFT$(S$.X-LEN(P$))+STR$(INT(A+.5)):X=X+Z:RETURN
92 '
93 ' SUB 94 ADVANCE ONE INTERVAL IN CYCLE
94 FOR K=0 TO M:U=0
95 FOR J=0 TO 2:U=U+(S(I.J)-S(I-1.J))*W(J.K):NEXT:U(I.K)=U
96 E=E(I.K):A(K)=(A(K)+U)*E:N(K)=N(K)*E:NEXT K:RETURN
98 END
```

```
200 DATA "DIRECT GAIN; 20 SQM 15 CM WALL; 20 SQM GLAZING
201 DATA 1500,3000,120,2,200,150,3
210 DATA "3-DAY CYCLE, SOLAR 75% TO WALL",6
211 DATA 8,0,9000,4000,0
212 DATA 16,0,0,1000,-6
213 DATA 8,0,900,1300,0
214 DATA 16,0,0,1000,-6
215 DATA 8,0,900,1300,0
216 DATA 16,0,0,1000,-6
220 DATA "3-DAY CYCLE, SOLAR 75% TO SPACE",6
221 DATA 8,0,3000,10000,0
222 DATA 16,0,0,1000,-6
223 DATA 8,0,300,1900,0
224 DATA 16,0,0,1000,-6
225 DATA 8,0,300,1900,0
226 DATA 16,0,0,1000,-6,"END"
```

```
DIRECT GAIN; 20 SQM 15 CM WALL; 20 SQM GLAZING
WALL:THERMAL MASS 1500 ; CONDUCTANCE 120
       OUTER & INNER SURFACE CONDUCTANCES 2   200
SPACE:THERMAL MASS 3000 ;CONDUCTANCE 150
 3 TIME CONSTANTS: 34.1  6.9   1
```

3-DAY CYCLE, SOLAR 75% TO WALL

TIME	SOURCES			AMB	TEMPS		
	OUT(WALL)IN	SPACE	TEMP		OUT(WALL)IN	SPACE
8	0	9000	4000	0	29	47	22
16	0	0	1000	-6	22	19	15
8	0	900	1300	0	20	20	15
16	0	0	1000	-6	14	12	9
8	0	900	1300	0	14	14	11
16	0	0	1000	-6	10	8	7

3-DAY CYCLE, SOLAR 75% TO SPACE

TIME	SOURCES			AMB	TEMPS		
	OUT(WALL)IN	SPACE	TEMP		OUT(WALL)IN	SPACE
8	0	3000	10000	0	17	29	27
16	0	0	1000	-6	19	17	14
8	0	300	1900	0	17	16	14
16	0	0	1000	-6	12	11	8
8	0	300	1900	0	11	12	11
16	0	0	1000	-6	9	8	6

```
0 CLS: PRINT "SUNSPEC: METRIC DATA:"'IBM PC. JULY 1986
1 '
2 DEF SEG=0:I=PEEK (&H417) OR &H40:POKE &H417,I:KEY OFF
3 DIM A(8,6),B(6),C(6),D(6),E(6),F(3),H(3,2),M(3)
4 DIM P$(2),Q(6),QM(3),R(6),S(6),T(8),T$(3,2)
5 DIM U(6),V(1,6,6),W(3),X(3,22),Y(3),Z(3)
6 '
7 AR$=":AREA": RET$=CHR$(13): ARSI$=AR$+RET$+"  RSI
8 WIN$=AR$+RET$+"  #PANES"+RET$+"  NIGHT RSI
9 P$(0)="SUNNY":P$(1)="AVGE ":P$(2)="COLD ": F(0)=700:F(2)=0
10 '
18 INPUT"  K(EY) OR FILENAME";D$: PRINT: IF D$="K" THEN 31
19 '
20 ' INPUT DATA FROM DISK FILE
21 OPEN D$ FOR INPUT AS #2: INPUT #2,Z,FP,FR
22 FOR J=0 TO 3: INPUT #2,M(J): NEXT
23 FOR I=0 TO Z: FOR J=1 TO I+19: INPUT #2,X(I,J): NEXT
24  FOR J=0 TO 2: INPUT #2,H(I,J): NEXT
25  IF I>0 THEN GOSUB 491: FOR J=1 TO I: A(K,J+1)=X(I,J+19): NEXT
26 NEXT I: CLOSE #2: GOTO 101
29 '
31 PRINT "INPUT DATA AS PROMPTED; MAIN LIVING ZONE LAST
32 PRINT "YOU MAY CORRECT ERRORS AFTER EACH PAGE
33 PRINT "THERMAL MASS: SCALE 1 - 4: NORMAL = 2": PRINT
34 INPUT "# ZONES";Z: Z=Z-1
39 '
41 FOR I=0 TO Z: ' BUILDING DATA FOR ZONES 0 TO Z
42  CLS: GOSUB 491
43  PRINT "ZONE";I+1;AR$;RET$;"2 WALL   ";ARSI$
44  PRINT "4 ROOF  ";ARSI$;RET$;"6 GROUND";ARSI$
45  PRINT "8 THERMAL MASS";RET$;"9 AIRCHANGES/HR
46  PRINT " WINDOWS FACING:";RET$;"11 SOUTH";WIN$
47  PRINT "14 NORTH";WIN$;RET$;"17 E & W";WIN$
49  '
51  IF I>0 THEN FOR J=1 TO I: PRINT"ZONE"J"BNDRY AREA/RSI ": NEXT
52  IF X(I,1)>0 THEN 71
59  '
60  ' INPUT BUILDING DATA
61  FOR J=1 TO I+19: IF J<>10 THEN LOCATE J,23: INPUT X(I,J)
62  NEXT: IF I>0 THEN FOR J=1 TO I: A(K,J+1)=X(I,J+19): NEXT
63  GOTO 81
69  '
70  ' PRINT BUILDING DATA
71  FOR J=1 TO I+19: IF J<>10 THEN LOCATE J,24:PRINT X(I,J)
72  NEXT
79  '
80  ' ALLOW BUILDING DATA CHANGES
81  INPUT"LINE# CHANGE OR N(EXT)";L$: L=VAL(L$)
82  IF L<1 OR L>I+19 THEN 86
83  GOSUB 261: X(I,L)=VAL(X$)
84  IF L>19 THEN A(K,L-18)=X(I,L)
85  GOTO 42
86 NEXT I
89 '
```

```
 91 CLS: PRINT"FOOTINGS:PERIMETER";RET$," RSI
 92 IF FP>0 THEN LOCATE 1,24: PRINT FP: LOCATE 2,24: PRINT FR
 93 L=1: GOSUB 261: FP=VAL(X$): L=2: GOSUB 261: FR=VAL(X$)
 99 '
100 ' SETUP NETWORK DATA
101 Y=.000001: O=Z+4: N=O+1: GE=FP/FR: A(O,1)=GE
102 FOR I=0 TO Z:A=X(I,1):X=0:U=0:W=0:V=0:GOSUB 491
103   FOR J=0 TO 2:L=11+3*J:G=X(I,L):R=X(I,L+1)/6+Y:W=W+G/R
104    V=V+G/(X(I,L+2)+R):U=U+X:X=X(I,2+2*J)/(X(I,3+2*J)+Y)
105   NEXT:E=16*X/FP:GE=GE+E:D=.8*X(I,9)*A+V
106   Y(I)=W-V:Z(I)=X(I,11)*(1-X(I,12)/9)+G/2
107   A(O,K)=D+U:A(K,1)=E:A(N,K)=X-E:C(K)=12*X(I,8)*A
108 NEXT I: M=Z+2: P=M+1: U=2*U: A(O,M)=U: A(P,M)=U
109 A(O,P)=D: C(1)=24*FP: C(M)=12*X(Z,8)*X(Z,2)
111 FOR I=1 TO P: D(I)=0: R(I)=SQR(C(I)): NEXT
112 FOR I=1 TO P: FOR J=I+1 TO N: G=A(J,I): D(I)=D(I)+G
113    IF J<O THEN D(J)=D(J)+G: V(1,I,J)=-G/R(I)/R(J)
114 NEXT J,I
115 FOR I=1 TO P: V(1,I,I)=D(I)/C(I):NEXT
119 '
120 ' COMPUTE MODAL PARAMETERS
121 FOR L=0 TO 1: M=P-L: GOSUB 501: NEXT
122 FOR I=1 TO M: FOR J=I+1 TO P: A(I,J)=A(J,I): NEXT J,I
123 O=P+1: IF NOT(D$="Z" OR D$="F") AND M(2)>0 THEN 211
129 '
130 ' CLIMATE/TEMP DATA PROMPTS
131 CLS: PRINT " 1 DESIGN TEMP": PRINT " 2 #HTG.MONTHS
132 PRINT " 3   DEG.DAYS": PRINT " 4 SUNSHINE HRS"
133 FOR I=0 TO Z
134   PRINT 5+3*I;"ZONE";I+1;": SHADE %
135   PRINT "   GAIN-WATTS": PRINT "   COMFORT TEMP"
136 NEXT: IF M(2)>0 THEN 161
139 '
150 ' INPUT CLIMATE/TEMP DATA
151 FOR J=0 TO 3: LOCATE J+1,23: INPUT M(J): NEXT
152 FOR I=0 TO Z: FOR J=0 TO 2
153   LOCATE 3*I+J+5,23: INPUT H(I,J)
154 NEXT J,I: GOTO 171
159 '
160 ' PRINT CLIMATE/TEMP DATA
161 FOR J=0 TO 3: LOCATE J+1,24: PRINT M(J): NEXT
162 FOR I=0 TO Z: FOR J=0 TO 2
163   LOCATE 3*I+J+5,24: PRINT H(I,J)
164 NEXT J,I
169 '
170 ' ALLOW CLIMATE/TEMP DATA CHANGES
171 INPUT"LINE# CHANGE OR N(EXT)";L$: L=VAL(L$)
172 IF L<1 OR L>7+3*Z THEN 211
173 GOSUB 261: X=VAL(X$)
174 IF L<5 THEN M(L-1)=X: GOTO 131
175 L=L-5: I=INT(L/3): J=L-3*I: H(I,J)=X: GOTO 131
179 '
```

```
200 ' SETUP DAILY SIMULATION DATA
211 W=(M(1)-1)/7: W(0)=1+W: W(2)=W: V=5*W: W(1)=V
212 F(1)=F(0)*(M(3)/240-W(0))/V: D=M(0)
213 E(0)=12+D/8: E(2)=D+5: T(N)=16+D/4
214 E(1)=(18*M(1)-M(2)/30-W(0)*E(0)-W*E(2))/V
219 '
220 ' INPUT TEMP SETBACK DATA
221 Y=.1: I=Z: CLS
222 PRINT "TEMP SETBACK: Y(ES) OR N(O)"
223 INPUT "6 NIGHT HRS ";N$: INPUT "8 DAY HRS    ";D$
224 IF N$="Y" OR D$="Y" THEN INPUT "SETBACK TEMP";TS
229 '
230 ' COMPUTE & PRINT DAILY SIMULATIONS
231 PRINT "DAILY TEMP. ZONE";I+1
232 PRINT "DAY\ HR 6AM 8  12   4PM 6   12
233 QM=0: S=0
234 FOR V=0 TO 2: IF Y>0 THEN GOSUB 311: I=Z
235   PRINT P$(V);T$(I,V)
236 NEXT: PRINT "PEAK AUX.KW";INT(QM(I))/1000
237 IF Y=0 THEN 243
238 Y=0: PRINT " ANNUAL KWHR";INT(S/33)
239 '
240 ' ALLOW OPTIONS AT END OF RUN
241 PRINT "TO ALTER ZONES, FOOTINGS, TEMP. SETBACK DATA;
242 PRINT "TO SEE NEW ZONE, FILEDATA, OR END;
243 INPUT "TYPE: Z, F, T, S; #, FILENAME, OR E";D$
244 I=VAL(D$)-1: IF D$="E" OR I>Z THEN END
245 IF I>=0 THEN 231
246 IF D$="Z" THEN 41 ELSE IF D$="F" THEN 91
247 IF D$="T" THEN 131 ELSE IF D$="S" THEN 221
249 '
250 ' FILE DATA ON DISK
251 OPEN D$ FOR OUTPUT AS #2: WRITE #2,Z,FP,FR
252 FOR J=0 TO 3: WRITE #2,M(J): NEXT
253 FOR I=0 TO Z
254   FOR J=1 TO I+19: WRITE #2,X(I,J): NEXT
255   FOR J=0 TO 2: WRITE #2,H(I,J): NEXT
256 NEXT I: CLOSE #2: GOTO 243
259 '
260 ' INPUT DATA FROM SCREEN SUBROUTINE
261 X$="": LOCATE L,23: INPUT S$
262 FOR C=24 TO 40: X$=X$+CHR$(SCREEN(L,C)): NEXT
263 RETURN
269 '
```

```
300 ' DAILY SIMULATION SUBROUTINE - 396
311 E=E(V): T=A(0,1)*E: FOR I=0 TO Z: GOSUB 491
312  T(K)=H(I,2): T=T+A(K,1)*T(K): T$(I,V)="": NEXT
313 T(1)=T/GE: M=P-1: T(M)=(T(P)+E)/2: T(0)=E
314 FOR K=1 TO M: Q=0: IF K=1 OR K=M THEN 317
315  FOR J=1 TO N: Q=Q+A(J,K)*(T(K)-T(J)): NEXT
316  I=K-2: G=H(I,1): QM(I)=Q-G: IF Q<G THEN Q=G: QM(I)=0
317  FOR J=P TO N: Q=Q+A(J,K)*T(J): NEXT: D(K)=Q: Q(K)=0
318 NEXT K: L=1
319 '
320 ' INITIAL STEADY STATE
321 FOR K=1 TO M: B=0
322  FOR I=1 TO M: B=B+V(1,I,K)*D(I): NEXT: B(K)=B/V(1,0,K)
323 NEXT K: GOSUB 411
329 '
330 ' DAILY SIMULATION, 6 TIME INTERVALS - 396
331 FOR IN=0 TO 5: READ H,L,TA: W=H*W(V): F=H(Z,2)
332  IF (L=1 AND N$="Y") OR (L=2 AND D$="Y") THEN F=TS
333  T(0)=E(V)+TA: D=F-T(0)
334  FOR I=0 TO Z: GOSUB 491: G=0
335   IF I<Z AND T(K)<H(I,2)+Y THEN G=QM(I): S=S+W*QM(I)
336   Q(K)=H(I,1)+G
337   IF L=2 THEN Q(K)=Q(K)+(1-H(I,0)/100)*Z(I)*F(V)-Y(I)*D
338  NEXT: Q=0: C=F-T(P)
339  IF ABS(C)>Y THEN L=0: GOSUB 421: GOTO 361
340 '
341  L=1: GOSUB 421: IF Q>0 THEN 386
342 ' AUX. HEAT KEEPS TEMP AT COMFORT TEMP. TC
349 '
350 ' IF Q<0, HEATGAIN ALONE KEEPS TEMP>TC
351  L=0: M=P: GOSUB 422: GOSUB 411: GOTO 391
361  HO=H: IF D<Y OR Q>0 THEN GOSUB 411: GOTO 386
371  IF ABS(D)<Y THEN GOSUB 411: H=HO-H: L=1: GOSUB 421: GOTO 386
379 '
380 ' FOR TI>TC>TF, FIND SUBINTERVAL WITH TF=TC
381  W=H*W/C/2: X=1+W-D/C: H=H/(X+SQR(X*X-X-W))
382  GOSUB 441: GOTO 371
384 '
386  S=S+Q*H*W(V): IF QM<Q THEN QM=Q: QM(Z)=Q
389 '
390 ' 391-3 STORE T(I) IN STRING FOR PRINTING
391  FOR I=0 TO Z: GOSUB 491
392   T%=T(K): T$(I,V)=T$(I,V)+" "+STR$(T%)
393  NEXT
394 '
396 NEXT IN: RESTORE: RETURN
399 '
```

```
410 ' COMPUTE TEMPS. T(I)
411 FOR I=1 TO M: A=0
412  FOR K=1 TO M: A=A+V(L,I,K)*B(K): NEXT: T(I)=A
413 NEXT I: RETURN
419 '
420 ' MOVE T(I) ON ONE TIME STEP -468
421 FOR I=1 TO P: S(I)=C(I)*T(I): NEXT: M=P-L
422 FOR I=1 TO M: A=Q(I)
423  FOR J=M+1 TO N: A=A+A(J,I)*T(J): NEXT: D(I)=A
424 NEXT I: IF L=1 THEN 461
429 '
430 ' STEP FOR MAIN TEMP FIXED (L=0) -455
431 D=F: FOR K=1 TO M: A=0: B=0
432  FOR I=1 TO M: U=V(L,I,K): A=A+U*S(I): B=B+U*D(I): NEXT
433  B=B/V(L,0,K): U(K)=A-B: D=D-U*B: R(K)=B
434 NEXT K: A=D: G=0: IF C>Y THEN 451
439 '
440 ' 441-3 TI<TC: 451-5 TI>TC
441 W=0: D=A: FOR K=1 TO M: T=V(L,0,K): B=EXP(-H*T)*U(K)
442  B(K)=R(K)+B: B=B*V(L,P,K): D=D-B: W=W+T*B
443 NEXT K: RETURN
449 '
451 FOR K=1 TO M: T=V(L,0,K): E=EXP(-H*T): B=E*U(K)
452  U=V(L,P,K): D(K)=(U-U*E)/T: D=D-B*U
453  B(K)=R(K)+B: G=G+U*D(K)
454 NEXT K: Q=D/G
455 FOR K=1 TO M: B(K)=B(K)+Q*D(K): NEXT: RETURN
459 '
460 ' STEP FOR MAIN TEMP VARYING (L=1)
461 FOR K=1 TO M: A=0: B=0
462  FOR I=1 TO M: U=V(L,I,K): A=A+U*S(I): B=B+U*D(I): NEXT
463  T=V(L,0,K): B=B/T: A=A-B: E=EXP(-H*T): X=(1-E)/T
464  B(K)=A*E+B: R(K)=A*X/H+B
465 NEXT K: Q=-Q(P)
466 FOR I=P+1 TO N: Q=Q+A(I,P)*(F-T(I)): NEXT
467 FOR I=1 TO M: A=0: B=0
468  FOR K=1 TO M: U=V(L,I,K): A=A+U*B(K): B=B+U*R(K): NEXT
469  T(I)=A: Q=Q+A(P,I)*(F-B)
470 NEXT I: RETURN
479 '
490 ' CONVERT ZONE #, I, TO NODE #, K
491 IF I=Z THEN K=Z+3: RETURN ELSE K=I+2: RETURN
499 '
```

```
500 ' EIGENMODE SUBROUTINE -567
501 FOR I=1 TO M
502  FOR J=I TO M: A(I,J)=V(1,I,J): NEXT: D(I)=A(I,I)
503 NEXT I
509 '
510 ' HOUSEHOLDER TRIDIAGONALISATION
512 FOR K=2 TO M: K1=K-1: AK=A(K1,K): A2=AK*AK: HA=0: IF K=M THEN 526
513  B(K)=0: FOR J=K+1 TO M: AKJ=A(K1,J): HA=HA+AKJ*AKJ: B(J)=0: NEXT
514  A2=A2+HA: B(K)=0: DS=0: IF HA=0 THEN 526
515  BK=AK: AK=-SGN(AK+Y)*SQR(A2): A(K1,K)=BK-AK: HA=A2-AK*BK
516  FOR I=K TO M: AKI=A(K1,I): BI=B(I)+A(I,I)*AKI: IF I=M THEN 518
517   FOR J=I+1 TO M:AIJ=A(I,J):BI=BI+AIJ*A(K1,J):B(J)=B(J)+AKI*AIJ:NEXT
518  B(I)=BI: DS=DS+BI*AKI
519  NEXT I:DS=DS/2/HA/HA
521  FOR J=K TO M: AKJ=A(K1,J): BJ=B(J)/HA-DS*AKJ: B(J)=BJ
522   FOR I=K TO J: A(I,J)=A(I,J)-A(K1,I)*BJ-AKJ*B(I): NEXT
523  NEXT J
526  S(K1)=HA: B(K1)=AK: E(K1)=A2/D(K1): D(K)=A(K,K)-E(K1)
527 NEXT K: ' SYMMETRIC FACTORS IN ARRAYS T & E
529 '
530 ' M UNSHIFTED LR STEPS, THEN SHIFT/RESTORE
531 K=M: DK=0: FOR I=1 TO M: GOSUB 581: NEXT
532 FOR K=M TO 1 STEP -1: IF K=1 THEN 535
533  DK=D(K): GOSUB 581: DK=-DK: GOSUB 581
534  IF ABS(E(K-1))>Y THEN 533
535  J=K: DK=D(K): IF K=M THEN 537
536  IF DK<D(J+1) THEN D(J)=D(J+1): J=J+1: IF J<M THEN 536
537  D(J)=DK:' EIGENVALUES IN DECREASING ORDER
538 NEXT K
539 '
550 ' TRIDIAG. EIGENVECTORS BY INVERSE ITERATION
551 FOR J=1 TO M: DJ=D(M-J+1): V(L,0,J)=DJ: EK=0
552  FOR K=1 TO M: QK=A(K,K)-DJ-B(K-1)*EK: IF ABS(QK)<Y THEN QK=Y
553   EK=B(K)/QK: E(K)=EK: Q(K)=QK: U(K)=1
554  NEXT K
555  FOR K=2 TO M: U(K)=U(K)-E(K-1)*U(K-1): NEXT: EK=0
556  FOR K=M TO 1 STEP -1: UK=U(K)/Q(K)-EK: U(K)=UK*Y
557   IF K>1 THEN EK=E(K-1)*UK
558 NEXT K:' EIGENVALUES & NORM'ED VECTORS IN ARRAY V
561  FOR K=M-1 TO 2 STEP -1: K1=K-1: HA=S(K1): IF HA=0 THEN 564
562   DS=0: FOR I=K TO M: DS=DS+A(K1,I)*U(I): NEXT: DS=DS/HA
563   FOR I=K TO M: U(I)=U(I)-DS*A(K1,I): NEXT
564  NEXT K
565  DS=0:FOR I=1 TO M:DS=DS+U(I)^2:NEXT:DS=SQR(DS)
566  FOR I=1 TO M: V(L,I,J)=U(I)/R(I)/DS: NEXT
567 NEXT J: RETURN
569 '
580 ' 581-3 LR-RECURSION RELATION
581 EK=DK
582 FOR J=1 TO K-1: D(J)=D(J)+E(J)-EK
583  E(J)=E(J)*D(J+1)/D(J): EK=E(J)+DK
584 NEXT J: D(K)=D(K)-EK: RETURN
589 '
599 DATA 6,1,-5,2,0,0,4,2,6,4,2,6,2,0,0,6,0,-3
```

A SAMPLE RUN OF SUNSPEC

```
SUNSPEC: METRIC DATA:
  K(EY) OR FILENAME? K

INPUT DATA AS PROMPTED; MAIN LIVING ZONE LAST
YOU MAY CORRECT ERRORS AFTER EACH PAGE
THERMAL MASS: SCALE 1 - 4; NORMAL = 2

# ZONES? 2


ZONE 1  :AREA           ? 100
2 WALL   :AREA          ? 40
  RSI                   ? 2
4 ROOF   :AREA          ? 0
  RSI                   ? 0
6 GROUND:AREA           ? 160
  RSI                   ? 2
8 THERMAL MASS          ? 4
9 AIRCHANGES/HR         ? .5
 WINDOWS FACING:
11 SOUTH:AREA           ? 2
  #PANES                ? 2
  NIGHT RSI             ? 2
14 NORTH:AREA           ? 1
  #PANES                ? 3
  NIGHT RSI             ? 0
17 E & W:AREA           ? 1
  #PANES                ? 2
  NIGHT RSI             ? 1
LINE# CHANGE OR N(EXT)? N


ZONE 2  :AREA           ? 140
2 WALL   :AREA          ? 170
  RSI                   ? 4
4 ROOF   :AREA          ? 100
  RSI                   ? 10
6 GROUND:AREA           ? 0
  RSI                   ? 0
8 THERMAL MASS          ? 2
9 AIRCHANGES/HR         ? .5
 WINDOWS FACING:
11 SOUTH:AREA           ? 8
  #PANES                ? 2
  NIGHT RSI             ? 2
14 NORTH:AREA           ? 1
  #PANES                ? 3
  NIGHT RSI             ? 0
17 E & W:AREA           ? 1
  #PANES                ? 2
  NIGHT RSI             ? 1
ZONE 1 BNDRY AREA/RSI ? 100
LINE# CHANGE OR N(EXT)? N


FOOTINGS:PERIMETER      ? 40
            RSI         ? 2
```

```
    1 DESIGN TEMP          ? -25
    2 #HTG.MONTHS          ? 8
    3  DEG.DAYS            ? 4200
    4 SUNSHINE HRS         ? 1000
    5 ZONE 1 : SHADE %     ? 5
     GAIN-WATTS            ? 400
     COMFORT TEMP          ? 16
    8 ZONE 2 : SHADE %     ? 0
     GAIN-WATTS            ? 800
     COMFORT TEMP          ? 20
LINE# CHANGE OR N(EXT)? N


TEMP SETBACK: Y(ES) OR N(O)
6 NIGHT HRS ? N
8 DAY HRS   ? N
DAILY TEMP, ZONE 2
DAY\ HR 6AM 8   12    4PM 6   12
SUNNY   20  20  24  28  26  23
AVGE    20  20  20  21  20  20
COLD    20  20  20  20  20  20
PEAK AUX.KW 4.639
 ANNUAL KWHR 10962
TO ALTER ZONES, FOOTINGS, TEMP, SETBACK DATA;
TO SEE NEW ZONE, FILEDATA, OR END;
TYPE: Z, F, T, S; #, FILENAME, OR E? 1
DAILY TEMP, ZONE 1
DAY\ HR 6AM 8   12    4PM 6   12
SUNNY   16  16  17  19  19  18
AVGE    16  16  16  17  16  15
COLD    16  16  16  16  16  16
PEAK AUX.KW 2.232
TYPE: Z, F, T, S; #, FILENAME, OR E? S


TEMP SETBACK: Y(ES) OR N(O)
6 NIGHT HRS ? Y
8 DAY HRS   ? N
SETBACK TEMP? 16
DAILY TEMP, ZONE 2
DAY\ HR 6AM 8   12    4PM 6   12
SUNNY   18  20  24  27  26  23
AVGE    17  20  20  21  20  20
COLD    16  20  20  20  20  20
PEAK AUX.KW 10.608
 ANNUAL KWHR 10302
TO ALTER ZONES, FOOTINGS, TEMP, SETBACK DATA;
TO SEE NEW ZONE, FILEDATA, OR END;
TYPE: Z, F, T, S; #, FILENAME, OR E? 1
DAILY TEMP, ZONE 1
DAY\ HR 6AM 8   12    4PM 6   12
SUNNY   16  16  17  19  19  18
AVGE    15  15  16  16  16  15
COLD    15  15  16  16  16  16
PEAK AUX.KW 2.232
TYPE: Z, F, T, S; #, FILENAME, OR E? E
```

```
1  '****** SOLRAD-MEAN SOLAR RADIATION   ON INCLINED SURFACE ******
2  '*****  BY C.CARTER, TRENT UNIVERSITY, ONTARIO, JUN 1986  *****
3  '
4  CLS: PRINT
5  PRINT"SOLRAD CORRELATES BEAM & DIFFUSE RADIATION WITH DAILY SUNSHINE
6  PRINT"HOURS OVER A MULTI-DAY INTERVAL; NUMBER DAYS FROM JANUARY 1.
7  '
11 PRINT "INPUT DATA AS PROMPTED:
12 PRINT "  LATITUDE, DEGREES (NORTH +)
13 PRINT "  INTERVAL: FIRST & LAST DAYS
14 PRINT "  MEAN DAILY SUNSHINE HOURS
15 PRINT "  GROUND ALBEDO - FRACTION
16 PRINT "  SURFACE: SLOPE FROM HORIZONTAL
17 PRINT "           ASPECT FROM SOUTH, DEGREES
18 PRINT
19 '
20 PI=3.14159
21 DR=PI/180: RH=24/PI: 'CHANGE DEGREES-RADIANS: RADIANS-HOURS
22 DO=23.45*DR: 'MAX SOLAR DECLINATION
23 IO=1367: 'SOLAR CONSTANT, WATTS/SQM
24 '
25 INPUT"LATITUDE, DEGREES";LAT: LAT=LAT*DR: CL=COS(LAT)
26 IF CL<.4 THEN PRINT "HIGH LATITUDE; MODEL INVALID": END
27 SL=SIN(LAT): TL=SL/CL: IF LAT=0 THEN TL=.000001
29 '
30 ' 2-PT GAUSSIAN INTEGRATION FOR INTERVAL MEANS
31 ' EC = ECCENTRICITY FACTOR; W = SUNSET ANGLE; DE = DECLINATION
32 INPUT "INTERVAL: FIRST DAY";JF
33 INPUT "         LAST DAY";JL: IF JL<JF THEN JL=JL+365
34 W=0: EC=1: JI=(JL-JF)*.2113
35 J=JF+JI: GOSUB 90: J=JL-JI: GOSUB 90
36 TD=-COS(W)/TL: CD=1/SQR(1+TD*TD): W=W-.1
37 DL=RH*W: PRINT "DAY LENGTH, HOURS";INT(100!*DL+.5)/100!
39 '
40 ' HORIZONTAL RADIATION: HO = EXTRA-TERRESTRIAL
41 '              HT = TOTAL, HD = DIFFUSE, HB = BEAM
42 CZ=CL*(SIN(W)-W*COS(W)): HO=RH*IO*EC*CD*CZ
44 '
45 INPUT "MEAN SUNSHINE HOURS";SH: FS=SH/DL
46 INPUT "GROUND ALBEDO, FRACTION";AL
47 HT=HO*(.18+.62*FS): HD=HT*(.79-.6350001*FS)
48 HB=HT-HD: FB=HB/HO
49 '                 SOLRAD - CONTINUED
```

```
49 '                    SOLRAD - CONTINUED
51 INPUT "SURFACE: SLOPE";BE: BE=DR*BE: CB=COS(BE): SB=SIN(BE)
52 INPUT "         ASPECT";GA: GA=DR*GA: U=SB*COS(GA): V=SB*SIN(GA)
53 X=CL*CB+SL*U: Y=TD*(SL*CB-CL*U): D=X-Y+1E-08
54 Z=V*V+(X+Y)*D: IF Z>O THEN 61
55 '
56 IF D>O THEN RB=0: GOTO 80: ' SUN NEVER ABOVE SURFACE
57 WR=W: WS=-W: GOTO 68: '        SUN NEVER BELOW SURFACE
59 '
60 ' WR,WS = SUNRISE, SUNSET ANGLES ON INCLINED SURFACE
61 Z=SQR(Z): WR=2*ATN((V+Z)/D): WS=2*ATN((V-Z)/D)
62 R=0: IF D<O THEN 72
63 '
64 '  D>O NORMAL, SUNRISE BEFORE SUNSET
65 IF WS>W  OR WR<-W THEN RB=0: GOTO 80
66 IF WR>W THEN WR=W
67 IF WS<-W THEN WS=-W
68 A=WR: GOSUB 99: R=Q: A=WS: GOSUB 99: R=R-Q: GOTO 76
69 '
70 ' D<O, SUNRISE ON SURFACE AFTER SUNSET; THERE CAN BE TWO
71 '       DAILY SUNSHINE INTERVALS ON A POLAR ASPECT IN SUMMER
72 IF WR>-W THEN A=WR: GOSUB 99: R=Q: A=WS: GOSUB 99: R=R-Q
73 IF W>WS THEN A=W: GOSUB 99: R=R+Q: A=WS: GOSUB 99: R=R-Q
74 '
76 RB=R/CZ/2: ' RB = INCLINED/HORIZONTAL BEAM RADIATION
79 '
80 PRINT "WTHR/SQM/DAY ON SURFACE:": HR=INT(HT*AL*(1-CB)/2)
81 H1=INT(HB*RB): H2=INT(HD*(FB*RB+(1-FB)*(1+CB)/2))
82 PRINT"BEAM";H1,"DIFFUSE";H2,"REFLECTED";HR,"TOTAL";H1+H2+HR
83 '
84 PRINT
85 INPUT "NEW DATA OR END? TYPE: L LATITUDE, I INTERVAL, S SURFACE, E END";
N$
87 IF N$="L" THEN 25 ELSE IF N$="I" THEN 32
88 IF N$="S" THEN 51 ELSE END
89 '
90 ' SUBROUTINE FOR DE, EC, W
91 IF J>300 THEN J=J-365
92 IF J<60 THEN K=PI/176: PD=79: PE=3: GOTO 94
93 K=PI/186: PD=80: PE=0
94 DE=DO*SIN(K*(J-PD)): EC=EC+K*COS(K*(J-PE))
95 C=TL*TAN(DE): W=W+ATN(SQR((1+C)/(1-C)))
96 RETURN
97 '
98 ' SUBROUTINE USED TO FIND RB
99 Q=X*SIN(A)+Y*A-V*COS(A): RETURN
```

A SAMPLE RUN OF SOLRAD

```
SOLRAD CORRELATES BEAM & DIFFUSE RADIATION WITH DAILY SUNSHINE
HOURS OVER A MULTI-DAY INTERVAL: NUMBER DAYS FROM JANUARY 1.
INPUT DATA AS PROMPTED:
  LATITUDE, DEGREES (NORTH +)
  INTERVAL: FIRST & LAST DAYS
  MEAN DAILY SUNSHINE HOURS
  GROUND ALBEDO - FRACTION
  SURFACE: SLOPE FROM HORIZONTAL
          ASPECT FROM SOUTH, DEGREES


LATITUDE, DEGREES? 45
INTERVAL: FIRST DAY? 1
          LAST DAY? 31
DAY LENGTH, HOURS 8.24
MEAN SUNSHINE HOURS? 8
GROUND ALBEDO, FRACTION? .2
SURFACE: SLOPE? 90
        ASPECT? 0
WTHR/SQM/DAY ON SURFACE:
BEAM 5966      DIFFUSE 872    REFLECTED 207              TOTAL 7045


NEW DATA OR END? TYPE: L LATITUDE, I INTERVAL, S SURFACE, E END? S
SURFACE: SLOPE? 90
        ASPECT? 20
WTHR/SQM/DAY ON SURFACE:
BEAM 5606      DIFFUSE 823    REFLECTED 207              TOTAL 6636

NEW DATA OR END? TYPE: L LATITUDE, I INTERVAL, S SURFACE, E END? E
```

Derivation of Important Equations

Although the solutions to the equations that form the basis of the calculations in the text may involve sophisticated mathematical techniques, deriving these equations involves an understanding of the physical situation and some elementary algebra. This should be well within the scope of the average reader with high school mathematics.

THE STEADY STATE FOR A TROMBE WALL (EQN 9.1)

We wish to find q, the average heat flow through the wall, in terms of the steady state inside and outside ambient temperatures (T_i and T_a, respectively), the constant thermal resistances (R_0, R_1, and R where the subscripts 0 and 1 represent the outside and inside surfaces of the wall), and Q, the average solar heat source to the outer surface. T_0, the outer wall surface temperature, is not known.

The heat flow through the wall is given by the standard heat conduction equation:

$$q = (T_0 - T_i)/(R + R_1) \ . \tag{A.1}$$

The heat flow from the outer wall surface to ambient is

$$(T_0 - T_a)/R_0 \ . \tag{A.2}$$

Because the heat source to the surface must equal the heat flowing away from the surface in both directions:

$$Q = (T_0 - T_a)/R_0 + q \ . \tag{A.3}$$

Solving for the unknown, T_0:

$$T_0 - T_a = [QR_0(R + R_1) + (T_i - T_a)R_0]/(R_0 + R_1 + R) \ . \tag{A.4}$$

Substituting Eqn (A.4) into Eqn (A.3) and solving for q:

$$q = (QR_0 + T_a - T_i)/(R_0 + R_1 + R) \ . \tag{A.5}$$

This is Eqn (9.1).

TIME VARIATIONS IN A NETWORK MODEL

For each node in the network, the rate of heat gained or lost by the thermal mass must equal the heat source Q plus or minus that which is gained or lost to all the other nodes through the walls, etc.

For example, for node 1:

$$C_1\dot{T}_1 = Q_1 + U_{12}(T_2 - T_1) + U_{13}(T_3 - T_1) + \ldots + U_{1N}(T_N - T_1) \qquad (A.6)$$

$$= Q_1 + U_{12}T_2 + U_{13}T_3 + \ldots + U_{1N}T_N - T_1(U_{12} + U_{13} + \ldots + U_{1N}) , \qquad (A.7)$$

where $\dot{T}$ is the rate of temperature change with time, C is the thermal mass in the node, U_{1J} is the heat transfer coefficient between nodes 1 and J, and Q_1 is the heat source to node 1.

More generally, for the kth node:

$$C_k\dot{T}_k = Q_k + [U_{k1}T_1 + U_{k2}T_2 + \ldots + U_{kN}T_N - T_k(U_{k1} + U_{k2} + \ldots + U_{kN})] ,$$

$$\text{where } U_{kk} = 0. \qquad (A.8)$$

If the vector $\mathbf{T} = (T_1, T_2, \ldots, T_N)$ and vectors $\mathbf{Q}$ and $\dot{\mathbf{T}}$ are defined in the same fashion (see Glossary — *vectors*), then Eqn (A.8) becomes

$$C\dot{\mathbf{T}} = \mathbf{Q} - G\mathbf{T} , \qquad (A.9)$$

where C is an $N \times N$ diagonal matrix with $C_1, C_2, \ldots, C_N$ along the diagonal, and G, the modified heat transfer matrix, has the series $(U_{k1} + U_{k2} + \ldots + U_{kN})$ as its diagonal entries G_{kk}; and $-U_{ij}$ as its off-diagonal entries G_{ij}. Equation (A.9) is solved in Appendix B.

STEADY-STATE NETWORK MODEL

Equation (A.9) of the time variation model can be applied to the steady state, but because there is no temperature variation with time, $\dot{\mathbf{T}} = \mathbf{O}$, where $\mathbf{O}$ is the zero vector. Therefore,

$$\mathbf{Q} - G\mathbf{T} = \mathbf{O} . \qquad (A.10)$$

By the rules of matrix arithmetic:

$$\mathbf{T} = G^{-1}\mathbf{Q} . \qquad (A.11)$$

Finding the temperatures at each node therefore involves the simple operations of inverting the matrix G and multiplying it by the vector $\mathbf{Q}$. For reasons of computational efficiency, the inverse matrix G^{-1} is not computed explicitly, but is obtained indirectly by a so-called triangular factorisation of G. (See any text in numerical linear algebra.)

Note that this is the steady-state solution to which the time dependent terms are added in the modal method of solving the time variation problem (Appendix B).

Mathematics of the
Modal Method

FOR A NETWORK

Given a network with N nodes, $\mathbf{T}$ and $\mathbf{Q}$ are the N-dimensional temperature and heat-source vectors; C is the positive diagonal thermal capacity matrix, G is the symmetric positive definite heat transfer matrix, with spectral radius $O(N^2)$. The diagonal entries G_{ii} are $U_{i1} + U_{i2} + \ldots + U_{iN}$, and the off-diagonal entries are $-U_{ij}$, where U is the heat transfer coefficient between nodes. The differential equations to be solved are

$$C\dot{\mathbf{T}}(t) = \mathbf{Q}(t) - G\mathbf{T}(t) \; . \tag{B.1}$$

These equations are known technically as stiff, and have the property that a change in $\mathbf{Q}$ causes a rapid transient change in $\mathbf{T}$. Most network programs solve the equations by an implicit finite difference method, using short time steps, whenever $\mathbf{Q}$ changes rapidly or instantaneously. The present program uses a spectral solution in terms of the eigenmodes of the heat transfer matrix.

Define a diagonal matrix D with the eigenvalues d_k in increasing order as its elements, and a square matrix X whose columns are the generalised eigenvectors, so that

$$GX = CXD, \text{ with orthonormality relation } X^TCX = I \; . \tag{B.2}$$

In terms of D and X:

$$G = CXDX^TC \text{ and } G^{-1} = XD^{-1}X^T \; . \tag{B.3}$$

Then

$$X^TC\mathbf{T} = X^T\mathbf{Q} - DX^TC\mathbf{T} \; . \tag{B.4}$$

In terms of the diagonal exponential decay matrix $E(t)$ with elements $\exp(-d_k t)$, the spectral solution of the differential equations over an interval during which $\mathbf{Q}$ is constant may be written in two ways:

$$\mathbf{T}(t) = X\{D^{-1}X^T\mathbf{Q} + E(t)(X^TC\mathbf{T}(0) - D^{-1}X^T\mathbf{Q})\} \qquad (\text{B.5})$$

or

$$\mathbf{T}(t) = G^{-1}\mathbf{Q} + XE(t)X^TC[\mathbf{T}(0) - G^{-1}\mathbf{Q}] \ . \qquad (\text{B.6})$$

Equation (B.5) is the pure spectral solution, whereas Eqn (B.6) is a mixed solution, in terms of the steady-state solution, $G^{-1}\mathbf{Q}$, and a series of decaying modes. Equations (B.5) and (B.6) are roughly equivalent computationally, but Eqn (B.6) does not require evaluation of any of the higher eigenvectors in X for which the decay element in $E(t)$ is negligible. Equation (B.6) is thus the preferred solution for problems in which a severely truncated partial spectrum gives adequate accuracy. Currently, SUNSPEC uses the pure spectral solution.

The spectral method requires $5N^3/3$ floating arithmetic operations (flops) for computation of the complete spectrum of eigenvalues and eigenvectors, and $3N^2$ flops per time step. In contrast, an implicit finite difference method requires $N^3/6$ flops for symmetric triangular factorisation of the implicit matrix, and $2N^2$ flops per time step. Our experience has shown that overall the spectral method can use time steps about four times longer than the finite-difference method. However, the use of the larger time step means that detailed temperature variations are not revealed. If this detail is needed, the spectral method is inappropriate, but often only an interval mean is needed over the larger time step. For example, the mean gives the total heat flows through the network, and can conveniently be evaluated with an extra N^2 flops per time step, by integrating the original differential equations to give

$$\bar{\mathbf{T}} = G^{-1}\mathbf{Q} - G^{-1}C[\mathbf{T}(t) - \mathbf{T}(0)]/t \ . \qquad (\text{B.7})$$

For the fairly small numbers of nodes used in SUNSPEC, overall the spectral method is about twice as fast as a finite-difference method.

The mixed solution using a partial spectrum of only M eigenvectors requires $5N^3/6 + MN^2$ flops for the spectrum evaluation, and $N^2 + 2MN$ flops per time step. Preliminary trials indicate that values of $M = 2$ or 3 will normally give adequate accuracy, and it should be possible to speed up SUNSPEC by about another factor of 2.

FOR A WALL

If we choose a unit of length so that the wall extends from $z = 0$ to $z = 1$, then with solar radiation intensities Q_0 and Q_1 at $z = 0$ and $z = 1$, respectively; total internal heat source Q_2; surface temperatures T_0 and T_1; exterior ambient temperature T_a; and interior temperature T_2, the temperature variation through the wall obeys the heat conduction equation

$$\frac{\partial^2 T}{\partial z^2} = \frac{C}{U}\frac{\partial T}{\partial t} \qquad (\text{B.8})$$

subject to boundary conditions:

$$-U\frac{\partial T_0}{\partial z} = Q_0 + U_0(T_a - T_0) \quad \text{at } z = 0 \ ; \qquad (\text{B.9})$$

$$U\frac{\partial T_1}{\partial z} = Q_1 + U_1(T_2 - T_1) \quad \text{at } z = 1 \ ; \qquad (\text{B.10})$$

and

$$C_2 \frac{\partial T_2}{\partial t} = Q_2 + U_1(T_1 - T_2) + U_2(A - T_2) \tag{B.11}$$

in the interior space.

U_0 and U_1 are the surface thermal conductances, U is the thermal conductance of the wall; C is the thermal capacity of the wall and C_2 is the thermal mass in the interior space.

Many analytic solutions for this type of problem are described and referenced in Carslaw and Jaegar (see Bibliography), although this particular boundary condition is not explicitly mentioned. The solutions can be written as the sums of the stationary state solutions $S(z)$, S_2 and two infinite series of exponentially time-dependent terms:

$$T(z,t) = S(z) + A_k \cos(a_k z - \phi_k) \exp(-a_k^2 tU/C) \tag{B.12}$$

and

$$T_2 = S_2 + A_k f_k \exp(-a_k^2 tU/C) \ , \tag{B.13}$$

where

$$S(z) = S_0(1 - z) + S_1 z \ . \tag{B.14}$$

Define $R = 1/U$; $R_0 = 1/U + 1/U_0$; $R_2 = 1/U_1 + 1/U_2$, then

$$S_0 - A = [(R_0 + R_2 - 1/U_0)Q_0 + R_2 Q_1 + Q_2/R_2]/U_0(R_0 + R_2) \ , \tag{B.15a}$$

$$S_1 - A = [Q_0/U_0 R_0 + Q_1 + Q_2/U_2 R_2]R_0 R_2/R_0 + R_2 \ , \tag{B.15b}$$

$$S_2 - A = [Q_0/U_0 + R_0 Q_1 + (R_0 + R_2 - 1/U_2)Q_2]/U_2(R_0 + R_2) \ . \tag{B.15c}$$

From the boundary condition (B.9):

$$\phi_k = \arctan(x_0/a_k) \ , \tag{B.16}$$

from Eqn (B.10):

$$a_k \sin(a_k - \phi_k) = x_1[\cos(a_k - \phi_k) - f_k] \tag{B.17}$$

and from Eqn (B.11):

$$f_k = x_2 \cos(a_k - \phi_k)/(1 - wa_k^2) \ , \tag{B.18}$$

where

$$x_0 = RU_0 \ ; \ x_1 = RU_1 \ ; \ x_2 = U_1/U_1 + U_2 \ ;$$

and

$$w = C_2/CR(U_1 + U_2) \ .$$

By Eqns (B.16)-(B.18):

$$\frac{\tan(a_k)}{a_k} = \frac{x_0 + x_1[1 - x_2/(1 - wa_k^2)]}{a_k^2 - x_0 x_1[1 - x_2/(1 - wa_k^2)]} \ . \tag{B.19}$$

The roots a_k of Eqn (B.19) can be obtained iteratively as functions of x_0, x_1, x_2, and w, using Newton's method. There is, in fact, one root in each interval $(k - 1)\pi$

to $k\pi$. The A_k coefficients in Eqns (B.12) and (B.13) are determined from the initial or continuity conditions. We must obtain solutions to these equations for a number of successive intervals, over each of which the thermal inputs and resistances are constant. One continuity condition can be applied at each interval change for every A_k included in the infinite series in Eqns (B.12) and (B.13). As pointed out by Carslaw and Jaegar, however, the higher terms in the series are rapidly decreasing transient terms which are significant only for short times after a change of conditions. For example, with $C/U = 30$ hr, $C_2 = 0$, and $X_1 = X_0 = 1$, every hour after a change of conditions, the $k = 2$ transient term decreases by a factor of 0.64, the $k = 3$ term by a factor of 0.24, and the $k = 4$ term by a factor of 0.05. For a solar daily cycle, in which radiation conditions and placing of movable insulation remain approximately constant over periods of several hours, we should expect to obtain sufficiently accurate results by retaining only a few terms in the series.

SOLRAD — **Theoretical Basis of Microcomputer Program**

This interactive program uses correlation formulae of Hay and Iqbal as published in Iqbal's book, *An Introduction to Solar Radiation*. Simplified formulae for solar declination D and solar eccentricity factor E and a 2-point Gaussian integration formula are used to calculate the mean values of D, E, and sunset angle W over a multiday interval. The mean extraterrestrial radiation on a horizontal surface is then calculated from:

$$H0 = (24/\pi) \cdot I \cdot E \cdot \cos D \cdot \cos L (\sin W - W \cdot \cos W) \qquad \text{(Iqbal 4.2.20)} ,$$

where I = solar constant, L = latitude,

$$W = \text{arc } \cos(-\tan D \cdot \tan L) \qquad \text{(Iqbal 1.5.4)} .$$

As recommended by Hay, the distorting effect of the period near sunrise and sunset can be excluded by reducing W. The program reduces W by 0.1 rad.

The mean daily bright sunshine hours S over the interval is input, and the mean total, diffuse, and beam radiations HT, HD, and HB on a terrestrial horizontal surface are calculated from the correlations.

$$HT = H0(0.18 + 0.62F) \qquad \text{(Iqbal 8.5.8)} ,$$

$$HD = HT (0.79 - 0.635F) \qquad \text{(Iqbal 8.10.11)} ,$$

$$HB = HT - HD = \text{direct beam radiation} ,$$

where

$$F = \text{mean daily fraction of sunshine hours}$$

$$= (\pi/24)S/W .$$

The mean radiation on an inclined surface with slope B from the horizontal, and aspect G from south, is taken to consist of the direct beam radiation $H1$, the diffuse radiation $H2$, and the ground reflected radiation HR. $H1$ is determined from

HB by a purely geometric relation. First the sunrise and sunset angles on the inclined surface are determined from

$$WR, \; WS = \frac{2 \arctan[V + (V^2 + X^2 - Y^2)^{1/2}]}{X - Y} \qquad \text{(Iqbal 1.6.16–17)} \; , \\ \text{reformulated}$$

where

$$U = \sin B \cos G \; ,$$

$$V = \sin B \sin G \; ,$$

$$X = \cos L \cos B + \sin L \cdot U \; ,$$

$$Y = \tan D(\sin L \cos B - \cos L \cdot U) \; .$$

Then, the ratio of the beam radiation on the inclined surface to that on a horizontal surface is

$$RB = \frac{(\sin WR - \sin WS)X + (\cos WS - \cos WR)V + (WR - WS)Y}{2 \cos L(\sin W - W \cos W)} \qquad \text{(Iqbal 4.4.18)} \; ,$$

so $H1 = HB \cdot RB$.

If the expression $V^2 + X^2 - Y^2$ inside the square root is negative, the sun never rises above the surface if $X > Y$, and never sets below it if $X < Y$. In the former case, $RB = 0$. In the latter case, sunrise and sunset are determined by the horizontal values, so set $WR = W$, $WS = -W$.

Generally, WR and WS must be compared against the horizontal values W and $-W$. When $X > Y$, sunrise on the inclined surface occurs before sunset. But, if $WS > W$ or $WR < -W$, the sun is above the inclined surface only when it is below the horizon, so $RB = 0$. When $X < Y$, the inclined surface sunrise occurs after its sunset. In this case, there may be two direct-beam radiation intervals per day on the surface in early morning and late afternoon. This occurs, for example, on a north-facing vertical surface in midsummer in northern latitudes. In this case, RB is given by the sum of two terms like Eqn (4.4.18), one with $WR = W$, $WS = WS$, the other with $WR = WR$, $WS = -W$. All these complications in calculating RB are not adequately described in Iqbal's book.

Hay's anistropic formula is used for diffuse radiation

$$H2 = HD[FB \cdot RB + (1 - FB) \cdot (1 + \cos B)/2] \qquad \text{(Iqbal 11.5.12)} \; ,$$

where $FB = HB/H0$.

Ground reflection is taken to be isotropic with ground albedo AL, so

$$HR = AL \cdot HT \cdot (1 - \cos B)/2 \qquad \text{(Iqbal 11.3.6)} \; .$$

Any radiation calculation based on correlation may sometimes be inaccurate, but SOL-RAD usually gives results accurate to within 10%. Because only mean daily sunshine hours are used, no distinction is made between morning and afternoon sunshine; hence eastward and westward aspects have the same computed radiations.

Specimen Building Plans

Plan D1 is a medium-sized passive solar family dwelling. All but one of the living rooms and bedrooms have a southern exposure, with 15 m² of south-facing windows admitting into five rooms. A two-storey-high sun space with 20 m² of windows and a below-ground rock store buffers the south exposure of the family room and main bedroom. Entrance, garage, and cold room are on the north. The long sloping north roof reduces the northern exposure, and there is minimal window area on north, east, and west.

Possible variants of this design might allow full-height south-facing windows in the basement-level recreation room, and small east windows in bedroom 3 and the dining room to admit the morning sun and improve daylighting. A small high-level west window would improve the natural lighting in the family room.

BASEMENT
1140 FT²   106 m²

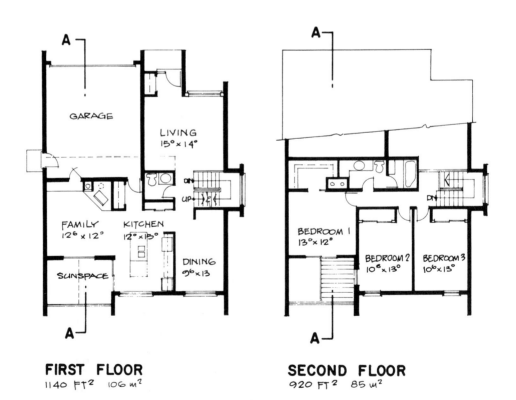

FIRST FLOOR
1140 FT²   106 m²

SECOND FLOOR
920 FT²   85 m²

FIG. D.1. Plan D1—medium-sized passive solar home

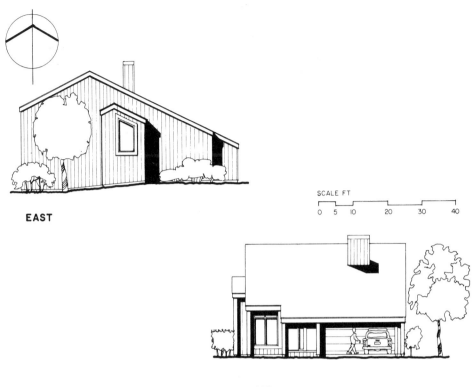

EAST

SCALE FT

0   5   10   20   30   40

NORTH

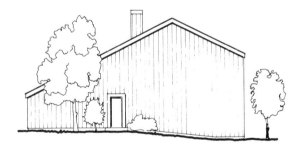

WEST

SOUTH

Plan D2 is a smaller passive solar home where all living rooms and bedrooms have a southern exposure. A large sun space adjoining the kitchen/dining area has 10 m^2 of window. A further 10 m^2 of south-facing window lets the sun into the living room and bedrooms, and through the high-level clerestory windows into the bathrooms and stairwell on the north side. There is one small east window in the kitchen, but no west windows at all. As with plan D1, some designers might wish to improve natural lighting with extra small windows on east and west.

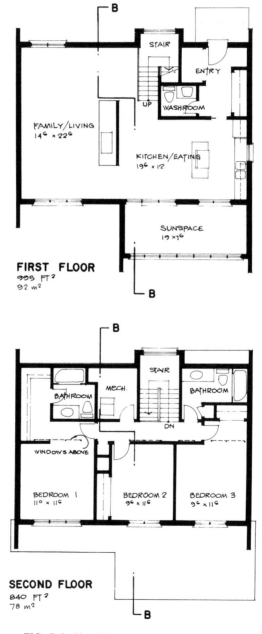

FIG. D.2. Plan D2—smaller passive solar home

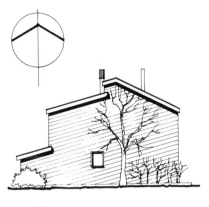

EAST

SCALE FT

NORTH

WEST

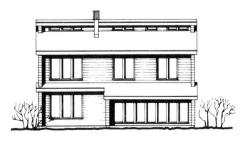

SOUTH

Plan D3 is a small, solar-tempered two-level home, with a total south-facing window area of 10 m². The more conventional design has limited opportunities for good exposure. Two bedrooms and the kitchen are on the north side, with only east- or west-facing windows. On a suitable site the basement-level recreation room might be given full height (or larger) south-facing windows.

FIRST FLOOR
960 FT²
89 m²

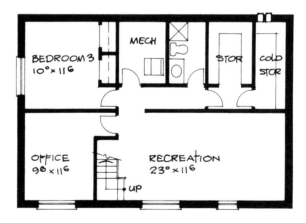

BASEMENT
960 FT²
89 m²

FIG. D.3. Plan D3 — small solar-tempered home

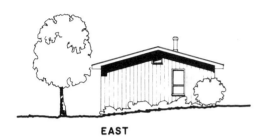

EAST

SCALE FT

0   5   10   15   20   25

NORTH

WEST

SOUTH

Plan D4 shows one level of a 24-unit three-storey block of solar apartments designed by Donald Watson and Buchanan Associates. This is an unusual solar design in that the axis is north–south, but the windows that would normally face east or west are reoriented to the south. This is an interesting idea, but in this particular design, much of the interior space is so far from the windows that artificial lighting would probably be needed much of the time.

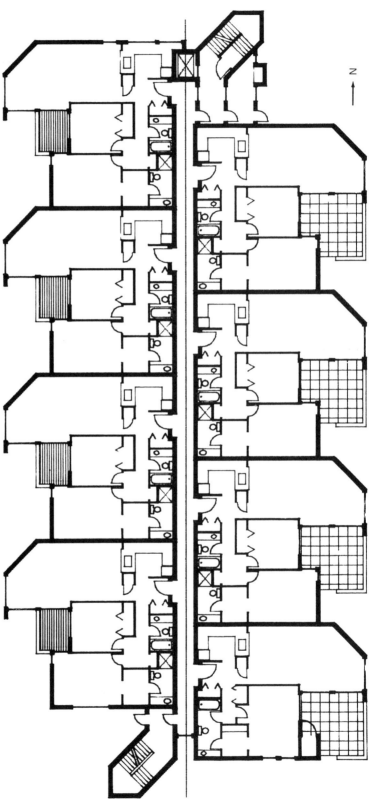

FIG. D.4. Plan D4—24-unit solar apartment block

Climatological Tables

COUNTRIES

CLEAR DAY RADIATION ON HORIZONTAL AND VERTICAL SOUTH SURFACES

H=Clear day radiation on a horizontal surface (w/sq.m.)

SV=Clear day radiation on a south-facing vertical surface (w/sq.m.)

		Jan	Feb	Mar	Apr	May	Jun	Jul	Aug	Sep	Oct	Nov	Dec
28°	H	191	241	287	319	339	343	328	314	277	236	190	172
	SV	205	177	120	65	48	47	49	63	116	170	201	208
32°	H	169	222	274	314	339	346	336	309	265	217	168	149
	SV	205	187	136	79	55	51	55	77	131	179	201	207
36°	H	147	202	259	306	338	348	335	303	251	198	146	126
	SV	204	194	151	95	66	59	65	91	145	185	199	201
40°	H	125	181	243	299	335	348	333	295	236	177	124	103
	SV	198	197	164	110	79	69	77	106	156	189	193	188
44°	H	101	159	226	289	332	347	330	286	218	159	101	80
	SV	187	198	174	125	93	83	91	120	167	189	182	170
48°	H	79	137	207	277	326	345	325	274	200	134	78	59
	SV	169	195	182	139	109	97	106	134	173	186	165	149
52°	H	57	114	188	264	320	341	319	262	181	113	57	39
	SV	146	190	188	152	124	113	121	146	178	180	142	121
56°	H	37	92	167	249	312	337	312	248	160	90	37	21
	SV	118	179	191	163	138	128	135	143	179	169	115	82

CANADA

DT - outdoor winter design temperature (celsius)
HDDC - heating degree days (celsius)
HS - monthly average solar radiation on a horizontal surface (w/sq.m.)
VS - monthly average solar radiation on vertical surface (w/sq.m.)
BSH (except USA) = # of bright sunshine hours (monthly total)
AT - ambient temperature

Churchill, Manitoba   DT -41 deg.   LAT 58 deg. 45'

	Jan	Feb	Mar	Apr	May	Jun	Jul	Aug	Sep	Oct	Nov	Dec
HDDC	1410	1240	1191	843	603	356	200	212	378	606	907	1246
HS	26	67	143	225	242	257	240	185	106	50	27	18
VS	106	169	241	246	176	156	155	153	122	87	80	86
BSH	80	132	189	204	195	234	285	232	111	62	50	55
AT	-28	-26	-20	-10	-2	6	12	11	5	-2	-12	-22

Edmonton, Alta.   DT -34 deg.   LAT 53 deg. 40'

	Jan	Feb	Mar	Apr	May	Jun	Jul	Aug	Sep	Oct	Nov	Dec
HDDC	1068	829	765	443	246	134	79	109	246	414	705	963
HS	43	82	145	202	239	254	262	211	147	90	47	31
VS	118	163	200	181	151	138	150	158	160	154	116	92
BSH	90	116	168	228	278	272	306	277	182	162	107	78
AT	-17	-11	-7	3	10	14	16	15	10	5	-6	-13

Fredericton, N.B.   DT -27 deg.   LAT 45 deg. 39'

	Jan	Feb	Mar	Apr	May	Jun	Jul	Aug	Sep	Oct	Nov	Dec
HDDC	839	744	636	420	233	82	20	37	145	319	491	755
HS	63	103	146	181	207	238	227	201	151	100	57	47
VS	126	163	156	129	112	113	113	127	134	125	89	96
BSH	107	124	140	154	200	206	233	221	167	138	95	93
AT	-9	-8	-2	4	11	16	19	18	13	8	1	-6

DT - outdoor winter design temperature (celsius)
HDDC - heating degree days (celsius)
HS - monthly average solar radiation on a horizontal surface (w/sq.m.)
VS - monthly average solar radiation on vertical surface (w/sq.m.)
BSH (except USA) = # of bright sunshine hours (monthly total)
AT - ambient temperature

Halifax, N.S.   DT -18 deg.   LAT 44 deg. 39'

	Jan	Feb	Mar	Apr	May	Jun	Jul	Aug	Sep	Oct	Nov	Dec
HDDC	680	627	573	409	264	107	27	20	101	255	398	602
HS	59	92	142	170	197	233	218	205	160	105	61	43
VS	102	129	144	119	105	107	108	125	138	129	93	73
BSH	93	118	140	165	207	203	226	217	182	154	95	85
AT	-6	-6	-2	3	9	15	18	18	14	9	3	-3

Montreal, Que.   DT -26 deg.   LAT 45 deg. 35'

	Jan	Feb	Mar	Apr	May	Jun	Jul	Aug	Sep	Oct	Nov	Dec
HDDC	851	731	624	373	164	41	7	20	103	288	482	746
HS	61	101	145	183	215	239	245	199	153	96	52	44
VS	114	151	149	130	113	110	119	123	135	121	83	83
BSH	96	117	164	187	233	242	265	232	183	140	74	78
AT	-10	-9	-2	6	13	18	21	20	15	9	2	-6

Moosonee, Ont.   DT   LAT 51.3

	Jan	Feb	Mar	Apr	May	Jun	Jul	Aug	Sep	Oct	Nov	Dec
HDDC	1190	1032	939	607	383	197	108	133	260	431	678	1054
HS	49	94	146	193	208	233	215	175	122	69	39	36
VS	113	183	210	192	149	151	133	150	158	124	83	87
BSH	82	122	148	173	197	219	237	215	120	88	51	59
AT	-20	-19	-12	-2	6	12	15	14	10	4	-5	-16

DT - outdoor winter design temperature (celsius)
HDDC - heating degree days (celsius)
HS - monthly average solar radiation on a horizontal surface (w/sq.m.)
VS - monthly average solar radiation on vertical surface (w/sq.m.)
BSH (except USA) = # of bright sunshine hours (monthly total)
AT - ambient temperature

Ottawa, Ont.   DT -27 deg.   LAT 45 deg. 25'

	Jan	Feb	Mar	Apr	May	Jun	Jul	Aug	Sep	Oct	Nov	Dec
HDDC	893	776	647	380	171	43	11	26	121	296	492	790
HS	67	109	159	193	230	248	248	210	155	101	54	51
VS	121	167	177	137	121	113	119	130	136	124	81	93
BSH	99	120	148	177	239	247	274	243	168	136	80	79
AT	-11	-10	-3	6	13	18	21	19	14	8	1	-8

Suffield, Alta.   DT -34 deg.   LAT 50 deg. 16'

	Jan	Feb	Mar	Apr	May	Jun	Jul	Aug	Sep	Oct	Nov	Dec
HDDC	979	757	681	387	200	82	25	43	167	341	610	825
HS	57	99	162	207	250	272	290	238	167	107	59	44
VS	146	185	208	168	148	135	152	166	171	169	131	123
BSH	98	126	180	210	278	286	351	306	208	185	122	88
AT	-14	-9	-4	5	12	16	20	18	13	7	-2	-9

Swift Current, Sask.   DT -34 deg.   LAT 50 deg. 20'

	Jan	Feb	Mar	Apr	May	Jun	Jul	Aug	Sep	Oct	Nov	Dec
HDDC	1017	802	702	421	234	92	35	58	194	374	655	877
HS	59	102	167	205	246	266	285	235	167	109	61	45
VS	150	192	218	168	143	132	149	163	170	173	134	124
BSH	92	122	162	192	273	275	331	292	183	160	107	83
AT	-15	-10	-6	4	11	15	18	18	12	6	-4	-10

DT - outdoor winter design temperature (celsius)
HDDC - heating degree days (celsius)
HS - monthly average solar radiation on a horizontal surface (w/sq.m.)
VS - monthly average solar radiation on vertical surface (w/sq.m.)
BSH (except USA) = # of bright sunshine hours (monthly total)
AT - ambient temperature

Toronto, Ont.   DT -19 deg.   LAT 43 deg. 40'

	Jan	Feb	Mar	Apr	May	Jun	Jul	Aug	Sep	Oct	Nov	Dec
HDDC	766	683	590	352	181	49	11	20	98	267	439	669
HS	70	106	149	204	224	242	257	220	163	105	54	49
VS	126	154	156	142	114	109	118	181	137	126	77	88
BSH	94	123	144	194	230	273	296	246	184	142	79	77
AT	-7	-6	-1	6	13	18	21	20	16	10	3	-4

Vancouver, B.C.   DT -9 deg.   LAT 49 deg. 11'

	Jan	Feb	Mar	Apr	May	Jun	Jul	Aug	Sep	Oct	Nov	Dec
HDDC	454	352	359	255	176	83	32	32	98	221	37	401
HS	33	66	116	173	238	250	266	215	155	84	41	26
VS	58	96	125	133	137	125	138	146	151	111	66	48
BSH	55	83	129	168	240	236	297	244	181	123	69	49
AT	3	5	6	9	11	15	17	17	14	10	6	4

Winnipeg, Manitoba   DT -35 deg.   LAT 49 deg. 50'

	Jan	Feb	Mar	Apr	May	Jun	Jul	Aug	Sep	Oct	Nov	Dec
HDDC	1155	949	811	439	219	70	21	43	178	370	676	992
HS	61	106	163	202	240	266	265	223	155	95	53	44
VS	154	199	209	165	139	131	140	152	154	138	104	116
BSH	121	144	176	220	266	276	316	283	185	152	91	93
AT	-19	-16	-8	3	11	17	20	18	12	6	-4	-14

USA

DT - outdoor winter design temperature (Celsius)
HDDC - heating degree days (celsius)
HS - monthly average solar radiation on a horizontal surface (w/sq.m.)
VS - monthly average solar radiation on vertical surface (w/sq.m.)
PBS - USA = percentage of possible bright sunshine (monthly)
AT - ambient temperature

Albuquerque, N.M.   DT -11 deg.   LAT 35 deg.

	Jan	Feb	Mar	Apr	May	Jun	Jul	Aug	Sep	Oct	Nov	Dec
HDDC	521	394	333	161	45	0	0	0	7	128	360	486
HS	133	176	232	293	334	352	327	301	259	203	149	122
VS	201	213	208	181	157	149	144	163	200	222	211	194
PBS	73	73	74	77	80	83	76	76	80	79	78	72
AT	2	4	8	13	18	24	26	25	21	14	7	2

Amarillo, Texas   DT -14 deg.   LAT 35 deg. 12'

	Jan	Feb	Mar	Apr	May	Jun	Jul	Aug	Sep	Oct	Nov	Dec
HDDC	491	372	306	141	31	0	0	0	10	115	319	446
HS	126	163	214	265	291	316	300	276	231	184	136	115
VS	191	199	193	165	138	134	133	151	180	202	194	183
PBS	69	68	71	73	73	77	77	78	74	75	73	67
AT	2	4	8	14	19	24	26	26	21	16	8	4

Atlanta, Ga.   DT -8 deg.   LAT 33 deg. 36'

	Jan	Feb	Mar	Apr	May	Jun	Jul	Aug	Sep	Oct	Nov	Dec
HDDC	356	290	240	82	14	0	0	0	10	69	234	363
HS	94	127	171	222	244	252	238	225	187	158	116	86
VS	137	148	147	131	111	104	102	117	138	165	158	136
PBS	47	52	57	65	69	67	61	65	63	67	60	50
AT	7	8	11	16	21	25	26	26	23	17	11	7

DT - outdoor winter design temperature (Celsius)
HDDC - heating degree days (celsius)
HS - monthly average solar radiation on a horizontal surface (w/sq.m.)
VS - monthly average solar radiation on vertical surface (w/sq.m.)
PBS - USA = percentage of possible bright sunshine (monthly)
AT - ambient temperature

Birmingham, Ala.   DT -8 deg.   LAT 33 deg. 36'

	Jan	Feb	Mar	Apr	May	Jun	Jul	Aug	Sep	Oct	Nov	Dec
HDDC	332	259	103	60	5	0	0	0	3	52	203	311
HS	93	127	170	220	244	252	238	227	191	160	113	87
VS	135	148	146	130	111	104	101	117	142	167	154	133
PBS	41	49	55	63	67	65	60	62	63	67	56	45
AT	7	8	12	17	22	25	27	26	23	17	11	7

Bismarck, N.D.   DT -31 deg.   LAT 46 deg. 48'

	Jan	Feb	Mar	Apr	May	Jun	Jul	Aug	Sep	Oct	Nov	Dec
HDDC	956	808	674	361	184	66	19	16	124	323	606	813
HS	61	102	154	192	243	271	287	147	178	119	67	49
VS	129	170	192	170	162	157	176	192	194	180	131	109
PBS	54	56	60	58	63	64	76	73	65	59	44	47
AT	-13	-10	-4	6	12	18	22	21	14	8	-2	-9

Brownsville, Texas   DT 2 deg.   LAT 25 deg. 54'

	Jan	Feb	Mar	Apr	May	Jun	Jul	Aug	Sep	Oct	Nov	Dec
HDDC	115	60	41	0	0	0	0	0	0	0	37	84
HS	120	149	192	228	253	278	291	266	223	189	139	113
VS	141	139	131	108	98	106	112	114	130	158	153	141
PBS	45	49	51	56	66	72	81	76	66	66	52	46
AT	16	17	20	24	26	28	29	29	28	24	20	17

DT – outdoor winter design temperature (Celsius)
HDDC – heating degree days (celsius)
HS – monthly average solar radiation on a horizontal surface (w/sq.m.)
VS – monthly average solar radiation on vertical surface (w/sq.m.)
PBS – USA = percentage of possible bright sunshine (monthly)
AT – ambient temperature

Boise, Idaho   DT -22 deg.   LAT 41 deg. 48'

	Jan	Feb	Mar	Apr	May	Jun	Jul	Aug	Sep	Oct	Nov	Dec
HDDC	623	478	404	245	137	45	0	0	74	232	443	570
HS	63	110	171	240	299	324	343	289	228	150	83	57
VS	122	169	197	193	181	171	191	203	227	207	148	116
PBS	41	52	63	68	71	75	89	85	82	67	45	39
AT	-2	2	5	9	14	18	24	22	17	11	4	0

Boston, Mass.   DT -14 deg.   LAT 42 deg. 20'

	Jan	Feb	Mar	Apr	May	Jun	Jul	Aug	Sep	Oct	Nov	Dec
HDDC	609	544	474	287	116	30	0	4	34	177	338	550
HS	62	93	134	174	213	239	230	195	165	117	66	53
VS	115	138	148	135	124	122	124	133	159	157	115	104
PBS	54	56	57	56	58	63	66	67	63	61	51	52
AT	-2	-1	3	9	15	20	23	22	18	13	7	1

Buffalo, N.Y.   DT -17 deg.   LAT 43 deg. 0'

	Jan	Feb	Mar	Apr	May	Jun	Jul	Aug	Sep	Oct	Nov	Dec
HDDC	641	582	581	361	184	44	11	21	79	246	647	703
HS	46	72	117	173	210	237	233	199	151	103	53	37
VS	86	108	131	136	124	123	127	137	148	140	93	74
PBS	34	40	46	52	58	66	69	66	60	53	29	27
AT	-4	-4	0	7	13	19	21	20	17	11	4	-2

DT - outdoor winter design temperature (Celsius)
HDDC - heating degree days (celsius)
HS - monthly average solar radiation on a horizontal surface (w/sq.m.)
VS - monthly average solar radiation on vertical surface (w/sq.m.)
PBS - USA = percentage of possible bright sunshine (monthly)
AT - ambient temperature

Burlington, VT.   DT -24 deg.   LAT 44 deg. 30'

	Jan	Feb	Mar	Apr	May	Jun	Jul	Aug	Sep	Oct	Nov	Dec
HDDC	847	746	665	700	198	50	16	36	116	302	499	755
HS	51	80	124	170	207	227	226	194	147	97	49	37
VS	99	125	145	141	128	123	129	140	151	138	91	77
PBS	42	48	52	50	56	60	65	62	55	50	30	33
AT	-8	-7	-2	6	13	18	21	19	15	9	3	-5

Charleston, S.C.   DT -4 deg.   LAT 32 deg. 50'

	Jan	Feb	Mar	Apr	May	Jun	Jul	Aug	Sep	Oct	Nov	Dec
HDDC	218	217	163	30	0	0	0	0	0	22	48	264
HS	98	131	176	228	244	242	236	208	183	157	123	95
VS	139	149	148	132	109	99	100	106	133	161	164	142
PBS	56	58	65	67	69	64	63	62	60	65	65	63
AT	9	11	14	18	22	26	27	27	24	19	13	9

Chicago, Ill.   DT -21 deg.   LAT 41 deg. 50'

	Jan	Feb	Mar	Apr	May	Jun	Jul	Aug	Sep	Oct	Nov	Dec
HDDC	677	584	498	269	118	27	0	0	45	183	422	623
HS	66	99	146	192	235	256	255	226	178	127	74	53
VS	121	145	159	146	134	132	135	151	168	168	127	101
PBS	44	47	51	53	61	67	70	68	63	62	41	38
AT	-4	-3	3	10	16	22	24	23	19	13	4	-2

DT - outdoor winter design temperature (Celsius)
HDDC - heating degree days (celsius)
HS - monthly average solar radiation on a horizontal surface (w/sq.m.)
VS - monthly average solar radiation on vertical surface (w/sq.m.)
PBS - USA = percentage of possible bright sunshine (monthly)
AT - ambient temperature

Cleveland, Ohio   DT -17 deg.   LAT 41 deg. 20'

	Jan	Feb	Mar	Apr	May	Jun	Jul	Aug	Sep	Oct	Nov	Dec
HDDC	649	586	514	309	146	40	5	14	59	215	413	609
HS	51	79	121	177	221	242	240	208	163	114	61	42
VS	92	114	131	134	125	120	125	137	152	149	104	80
PBS	32	37	44	53	59	65	68	64	60	55	31	26
AT	-3	-2	2	9	14	20	22	21	18	12	6	-1

Detroit, Mich.   DT -16 deg.   LAT 42 deg. 20'

	Jan	Feb	Mar	Apr	May	Jun	Jul	Aug	Sep	Oct	Nov	Dec
HDDC	661	592	524	292	123	24	0	0	49	202	413	609
HS	55	90	181	184	226	245	241	207	165	115	63	45
VS	101	133	146	143	131	125	130	141	158	154	109	88
PBS	32	43	49	52	59	65	70	65	61	56	35	32
AT	-3	-3	2	9	14	21	23	22	18	12	5	-1

Dodge City, Kans.   DT -18 deg.   LAT 37 deg. 50'

	Jan	Feb	Mar	Apr	May	Jun	Jul	Aug	Sep	Oct	Nov	Dec
HDDC	589	470	402	198	69	5	0	0	18	141	373	526
HS	109	147	194	248	275	310	302	270	222	171	118	96
VS	177	193	189	167	140	140	142	159	186	202	180	165
PBS	68	64	67	69	68	75	78	77	76	75	69	55
AT	-1	2	5	12	18	23	26	26	21	14	6	1

DT - outdoor winter design temperature (Celsius)
HDDC - heating degree days (celsius)
HS - monthly average solar radiation on a horizontal surface (w/sq.m.)
VS - monthly average solar radiation on vertical surface (w/sq.m.)
PBS - USA = percentage of possible bright sunshine (monthly)
 AT - ambient temperature

Great Falls, Mont.   DT -29 deg.   LAT 47 deg. 30'

	Jan	Feb	Mar	Apr	May	Jun	Jul	Aug	Sep	Oct	Nov	Dec
HDDC	755	646	595	359	213	104	16	30	144	304	516	655
HS	55	95	154	196	243	276	306	254	181	122	65	44
VS	118	161	196	177	165	164	192	202	202	187	131	100
PBS	49	57	67	62	64	65	81	78	68	61	46	46
AT	-6	-3	-1	6	12	16	21	19	14	9	2	-3

Houston, Texas   DT -3 deg.   LAT 29 deg. 40'

	Jan	Feb	Mar	Apr	May	Jun	Jul	Aug	Sep	Oct	Nov	Dec
HDDC	715	161	108	20	0	0	0	0	0	3	102	172
HS	101	136	170	200	233	249	240	222	193	168	121	96
VS	133	143	132	106	98	98	96	105	128	159	150	133
PBS	41	54	48	51	57	63	68	61	57	61	58	69
AT	11	13	16	21	24	27	28	28	26	22	16	13

Indianapolis, Ind.   DT -19 deg.   LAT 39 deg. 40'

	Jan	Feb	Mar	Apr	May	Jun	Jul	Aug	Sep	Oct	Nov	Dec
HDDC	623	531	453	242	99	22	0	0	50	177	405	589
HS	65	98	136	184	222	246	237	216	174	128	76	55
VS	112	135	140	131	119	116	118	135	155	160	123	99
PBS	41	51	51	55	61	68	70	71	66	64	42	39
AT	-2	-1	4	11	17	22	24	23	19	13	6	-1

DT - outdoor winter design temperature (Celsius)
HDDC - heating degree days (celsius)
HS - monthly average solar radiation on a horizontal surface (w/sq.m.)
VS - monthly average solar radiation on vertical surface (w/sq.m.)
PBS - USA = percentage of possible bright sunshine (monthly)
AT - ambient temperature

Kansas City, Mo.   DT -17 deg.   LAT 39 deg. 1'

	Jan	Feb	Mar	Apr	May	Jun	Jul	Aug	Sep	Oct	Nov	Dec
HDDC	478	458	382	165	61	0	0	0	22	123	343	507
HS	85	118	158	207	246	273	276	245	191	144	97	74
VS	144	160	161	146	131	128	136	151	168	177	155	132
PBS	64	54	61	65	67	72	84	69	51	62	46	54
AT	-3	0	5	12	18	23	26	25	20	14	6	-1

Los Angeles, CA   DT 5 deg.   LAT 34 deg. 0'

	Jan	Feb	Mar	Apr	May	Jun	Jul	Aug	Sep	Oct	Nov	Dec
HDDC	208	169	161	122	88	45	16	16	24	44	101	163
HS	122	160	212	256	271	279	303	273	221	173	132	111
VS	178	187	185	154	124	116	131	143	165	183	182	172
PBS	69	72	73	70	66	65	82	83	79	73	74	71
AT	13	13	14	15	17	18	21	21	18	16	14	

Memphis, Tenn.   DT -11 deg.   LAT 35 deg. 0'

	Jan	Feb	Mar	Apr	May	Jun	Jul	Aug	Sep	Oct	Nov	Dec
HDDC	408	327	255	82	12	0	0	0	10	73	250	391
HS	90	124	168	215	248	269	259	240	193	158	107	83
VS	135	150	151	133	117	114	114	130	149	173	152	132
PBS	48	54	57	63	69	73	72	75	69	71	58	49
AT	5	7	11	17	22	26	28	27	23	17	11	6

DT - outdoor winter design temperature (Celsius)
HDDC - heating degree days (celsius)
HS - monthly average solar radiation on a horizontal surface (w/sq.m.)
VS - monthly average solar radiation on vertical surface (w/sq.m.)
PBS - USA = percentage of possible bright sunshine (monthly)
AT - ambient temperature

Minneapolis, Minn.   DT -27 deg.   LAT 44 deg. 5'

	Jan	Feb	Mar	Apr	May	Jun	Jul	Aug	Sep	Oct	Nov	Dec
HDDC	913	772	653	348	161	45	12	17	106	282	568	814
HS	61	100	145	190	228	253	259	222	165	113	63	46
VS	121	159	172	159	144	139	150	163	170	162	118	98
PBS	51	57	54	55	58	63	70	67	61	57	39	40
AT	-11	-8	-2	7	14	19	22	21	16	10	0	-7

Shreveport, LA.   DT -7 deg.   LAT 32 deg. 3'

	Jan	Feb	Mar	Apr	May	Jun	Jul	Aug	Sep	Oct	Nov	Dec
HDDC	309	238	170	45	0	0	0	0	0	84	166	262
HS	100	136	176	212	248	271	265	247	204	171	122	96
VS	141	154	147	122	110	110	111	124	146	174	162	142
PBS	50	54	58	55	64	72	73	71	70	72	62	52
AT	8	11	14	19	23	28	28	25	20	13	9	

New York City   DT -12 deg.   LAT 40 deg. 5'

	Jan	Feb	Mar	Apr	May	Jun	Jul	Aug	Sep	Oct	Nov	Dec
HDDC	576	523	456	269	94	7	0	0	9	139	316	522
HS	66	95	136	179	215	225	222	195	160	118	70	53
VS	116	134	145	133	119	110	114	126	147	151	116	99
PBS	50	55	56	59	61	64	65	64	63	61	52	49
AT	0	1	5	11	17	22	25	24	20	15	8	2

DT – outdoor winter design temperature (Celsius)
HDDC – heating degree days (celsius)
HS – monthly average solar radiation on a horizontal surface (w/sq.m.)
VS – monthly average solar radiation on vertical surface (w/sq.m.)
PBS – USA = percentage of possible bright sunshine (monthlv)
AT – ambient temperature

Oklahoma City, Okla   DT –13 deg.   LAT 35 deg. 2'

	Jan	Feb	Mar	Apr	May	Jun	Jul	Aug	Sep	Oct	Nov	Dec
HDDC	486	371	295	106	19	0	0	0	8	92	279	429
HS	105	139	184	227	252	282	280	256	204	162	118	95
VS	160	170	167	142	120	121	124	140	160	179	170	153
PBS	59	61	63	63	65	73	75	77	69	68	60	59
AT	3	5	9	16	20	25	28	27	23	17	9	4

Phoenix, Arizona   DT –1 deg.   LAT 33 deg. 3'

	Jan	Feb	Mar	Apr	May	Jun	Jul	Aug	Sep	Oct	Nov	Dec
HDDC	265	184	122	42	0	0	0	0	0	12	131	232
HS	134	181	238	310	352	360	327	301	265	207	151	123
VS	193	209	204	182	159	148	139	156	195	216	205	187
PBS	78	80	83	89	93	94	85	85	89	88	83	77
AT	11	13	16	20	24	29	33	32	29	22	16	12

Pittsburgh, Penn.   DT –17 deg.   LAT 40 deg. 3'

	Jan	Feb	Mar	Apr	May	Jun	Jul	Aug	Sep	Oct	Nov	Dec
HDDC	550	495	427	218	69	7	0	0	34	163	344	520
HS	56	82	124	173	210	232	222	198	159	118	66	46
VS	98	116	130	127	116	112	113	127	145	150	132	85
PBS	36	38	45	48	53	60	62	60	60	56	40	30
AT	-2	-2	3	10	16	21	22	21	18	12	5	-1

DT - outdoor winter design temperature (Celsius)
HDDC - heating degree days (celsius)
HS - monthly average solar radiation on a horizontal surface (w/sq.m.)
VS - monthly average solar radiation on vertical surface (w/sq.m.)
PBS - USA = percentage of possible bright sunshine (monthly)
AT - ambient temperature

Portland, Maine   DT -21 deg.   LAT 43 deg. 4'

	Jan	Feb	Mar	Apr	May	Jun	Jul	Aug	Sep	Oct	Nov	Dec
HDDC	749	662	583	378	208	62	7	30	109	285	448	680
HS	59	90	128	171	206	225	218	192	152	108	60	43
VS	113	137	146	138	124	119	121	135	152	150	108	97
PBS	55	59	56	56	56	60	64	65	61	58	47	53
AT	-6	-5	0	6	12	17	20	19	15	9	4	-3

Raleigh, N.C.   DT -9 deg.   LAT 35 deg. 50'

	Jan	Feb	Mar	Apr	May	Jun	Jul	Aug	Sep	Oct	Nov	Dec
HDDC	406	345	272	101	19	0	0	0	12	92	252	401
HS	91	124	168	216	238	245	233	212	181	145	107	84
VS	141	154	154	137	115	106	105	118	144	162	155	136
PBS	5	58	63	64	60	61	61	61	60	63	63	56
AT	5	6	9	16	19	23	26	25	22	16	10	5

Salt Lake City, Utah   DT -16 deg.   LAT 40 deg. 50'

	Jan	Feb	Mar	Apr	May	Jun	Jul	Aug	Sep	Oct	Nov	Dec
HDDC	652	509	427	257	130	47	0	0	45	235	475	606
HS	84	130	191	249	310	337	340	296	242	170	104	75
VS	148	184	203	184	172	164	175	192	222	218	172	140
PBS	47	55	64	66	73	78	84	83	84	73	54	44
AT	-2	1	4	9	14	19	25	24	18	11	4	-1

DT - outdoor winter design temperature (Celsius)
HDDC - heating degree days (celsius)
HS - monthly average solar radiation on a horizontal surface (w/sq.m.)
VS - monthly average solar radiation on vertical surface (w/sq.m.)
PBS - USA = percentage of possible bright sunshine (monthly)
AT - ambient temperature

San Francisco, CA   DT 2 deg.   LAT 37 deg. 40'

	Jan	Feb	Mar	Apr	May	Jun	Jul	Aug	Sep	Oct	Nov	Dec
HDDC	284	221	203	156	130	70	45	44	33	80	171	259
HS	93	133	191	252	293	312	314	278	229	161	108	84
VS	151	172	185	169	148	140	148	163	191	189	164	144
PBS	56	62	69	73	62	73	66	65	72	70	62	53
AT	9	11	12	13	14	17	17	17	18	16	13	10

Seattle-Taloma, Wash.   DT -21 deg.   LAT 47 deg. 30'

	Jan	Feb	Mar	Apr	May	Jun	Jul	Aug	Sep	Oct	Nov	Dec
HDDC	464	380	370	265	165	89	31	35	91	219	355	420
HS	34	65	112	170	225	237	295	212	151	86	44	28
VS	73	111	142	153	153	140	185	168	167	132	89	63
PBS	21	42	49	51	58	54	67	65	61	42	27	17
AT	3	6	7	9	13	16	18	18	16	11	7	5

Tampa, Florida   DT 2 deg.   LAT 28 deg. 0'

	Jan	Feb	Mar	Apr	May	Jun	Jul	Aug	Sep	Oct	Nov	Dec
HDDC	113	83	57	0	0	0	0	0	0	0	34	96
HS	133	165	210	251	263	243	230	217	196	177	146	123
VS	165	164	152	126	106	93	90	97	122	158	170	161
PBS	66	67	70	73	75	66	60	59	60	63	67	64
AT	16	17	19	22	25	27	28	28	27	24	19	17

DT – outdoor winter design temperature (Celsius)
HDDC – heating degree days (celsius)
HS – monthly average solar radiation on a horizontal surface (w/sq.m.)
VS – monthly average solar radiation on vertical surface (w/sq.m.)
PBS – USA = percentage of possible bright sunshine (monthly)
AT – ambient temperature

Washington, D.C.   DT –10 deg.   LAT 38 deg. 50'

	Jan	Feb	Mar	Apr	May	Jun	Jul	Aug	Sep	Oct	Nov	Dec
HDDC	488	427	350	161	41	0	0	0	13	122	391	467
HS	75	107	148	192	226	250	239	213	176	132	86	63
VS	126	144	149	134	119	116	116	130	153	160	135	112
PBS	48	51	55	56	58	64	62	62	62	60	53	47
AT	0	1	6	12	17	22	24	23	19	13	7	1

AUSTRALIA

DT - outdoor winter design temperature (celsius)
HDDC - heating degree days (celsius)
HS - monthly average solar radiation on a horizontal surface (w/sq.m.)
BSH = # of bright sunshine hours (montly total)
AT - ambient temperature

Alice Springs, Australia

DT: 5.6 deg   LAT: 33 deg 52'S

	Jan	Feb	Mar	Apr	May	Jun	Jul	Aug	Sep	Oct	Nov	Dec
HDDC	0	0	0	0	84	171	198	115	0	0	0	0
HS	301	298	275	224	185	174	188	227	266	288	303	306
BSH	319	291	288	276	248	240	276	304	300	300	313	310
AT	28.1	27.5	24.7	19.8	15.3	12.3	11.6	14.3	18.2	22.8	25.5	27.4

Melbourne, Australia

DT: 3.4 deg   LAT: 37 deg 49' S

	Jan	Feb	Mar	Apr	May	Jun	Jul	Aug	Sep	Oct	Nov	Dec
HDDC	0	0	0	87	171	234	260	233	168	115	54	0
HS	283	244	190	131	87	75	78	112	157	204	238	264
BSH	242	207	202	150	127	102	115	143	165	180	186	217
AT	19.9	19.7	18.4	15.1	12.5	10.2	9.6	10.5	12.4	14.3	16.2	18.4

Perth, Australia

DT: 5.6 deg   LAT: 31 deg 57' S

	Jan	Feb	Mar	Apr	May	Jun	Jul	Aug	Sep	Oct	Nov	Dec
HDDC	0	0	0	0	59	129	152	140	99	52	0	0
HS	315	292	239	169	125	106	114	156	207	261	307	326
BSH	322	280	273	219	180	144	164	189	213	251	291	322
AT	23.4	23.9	22.2	19.2	16.1	13.7	13.1	13.5	14.7	16.3	19.2	21.5

DT - outdoor winter design temperature (celsius)
HDDC - heating degree days (celsius)
HS - monthly average solar radiation on a horizontal surface (w/sq.m.)
BSH = # of bright sunshine hours (montly total)
AT - ambient temperature

Sydney, Australia

DT: 5.6 deg   LAT: 33 deg 52'S

	Jan	Feb	Mar	Apr	May	Jun	Jul	Aug	Sep	Oct	Nov	Dec
HDDC	0	0	0	0	90	156	192	155	84	12	0	0
HS	260	220	212	154	124	104	122	153	191	249	283	268
BSH	226	185	195	183	180	189	189	214	216	229	228	229
AT	22	21.9	20.8	18.3	15.1	12.8	11.8	13.0	15.2	12.6	19.5	21.1

NEW ZEALAND

DT - outdoor winter design temperature (celsius)
HDDC - heating degree days (celsius)
HS - monthly average solar radiation on a horizontal surface (w/sq.m.)
BSH = # of bright sunshine hours (montly total)
AT - ambient temperature

Auckland, New Zealand

DT: 5.6 deg   LAT: 36 deg 51'S

	Jan	Feb	Mar	Apr	May	Jun	Jul	Aug	Sep	Oct	Nov	Dec
HDDC	0	0	0	48	130	186	223	208	162	115	63	9.3
HS	272	253	188	134	96	78	96	118	149	188	246	276
BSH	239	227	189	156	149	126	158	152	147	174	213	242
AT	19.2	19.6	18.4	16.4	13.8	11.8	10.8	11.3	12.6	14.3	15.9	17.7

Christchurch, New Zealand

DT: -0.6 deg   LAT: 43 deg 32'S

	Jan	Feb	Mar	Apr	May	Jun	Jul	Aug	Sep	Oct	Nov	Dec
HDDC	50	50	105	180	288	351	381	344	258	195	136	80
HS	232	211	146	104	65	50	58	84	134	193	227	251
BSH	198	196	161	162	124	123	124	136	153	192	195	211
AT	16.4	16.2	14.6	12.0	8.7	6.3	5.7	6.9	9.4	11.7	13.6	15.4

Wellington, New Zealand

DT: 2.8 deg   LAT: 41 deg 17'S

	Jan	Feb	Mar	Apr	May	Jun	Jul	Aug	Sep	Oct	Nov	Dec
HDDC	56	45	81	135	220	276	307	285	234	195	141	90
HS	247	233	170	123	73	63	68	92	145	201	245	273
BSH	229	213	186	159	115	111	121	121	126	192	207	226
AT	16.2	16.4	15.4	13.5	10.9	8.8	8.1	8.8	10.2	11.7	13.3	15.1

EUROPE

DT - outdoor winter design temperature (celsius)
HDDC - heating degree days (celsius)
HS - monthly average solar radiation on a horizontal surface (w/sq.m.)
BSH = # of bright sunshine hours (montly total)
AT - ambient temperature

Vienna, Austria

DT: -11.8 deg   LAT: 48 deg 15'

	Jan	Feb	Mar	Apr	May	Jun	Jul	Aug	Sep	Oct	Nov	Dec
HDDC	570	501	422	243	112	0	0	0	81	248	393	496
HS	28	54	105	156	213	217	225	191	139	91	47	28
BSH	40	53	112	159	233	210	254	229	174	155	90	56
AT	-0.4	0.1	4.4	9.9	14.4	18.0	19.9	19.2	15.3	10.0	4.9	2.0

Brussels, Belgium

DT: -7.3 deg   LAT: 50 deg 48'

	Jan	Feb	Mar	Apr	May	Jun	Jul	Aug	Sep	Oct	Nov	Dec
HDDC	493	414	394	264	167	60	34	40	93	211	363	496
HS	27	52	92	143	191	205	193	170	126	72	35	21
BSH	47	70	109	150	186	195	189	189	156	109	60	43
AT	2.1	3.2	5.3	9.2	12.6	16.0	16.9	16.7	14.9	11.2	5.9	2.0

Copenhagen, Denmark

DT: -28.6 deg   LAT: 55 deg 41'

	Jan	Feb	Mar	Apr	May	Jun	Jul	Aug	Sep	Oct	Nov	Dec
HDDC	561	507	490	342	205	48	47	47	117	242	378	524
HS	17	44	96	162	211	250	219	187	117	61	26	15
BSH	28	62	127	186	236	285	251	251	162	99	57	37
TA	-0.1	-0.1	2.2	6.6	11.4	16.4	16.5	16.5	14.1	10.2	5.4	1.1

DT – outdoor winter design temperature (celsius)
HDDC – heating degree days (celsius)
HS – monthly average solar radiation on a horizontal surface (w/sq.m.)
BSH = # of bright sunshine hours (montly total)
AT – ambient temperature

Berlin, East Germany

DT: –11.2 deg   LAT: 52 deg 28'

	Jan	Feb	Mar	Apr	May	Jun	Jul	Aug	Sep	Oct	Nov	Dec
HDDC	601	420	459	264	143	0	0	3	93	233	409	570
HS	25	47	101	145	199	227	219	190	127	66	32	19
BSH	43	62	136	150	208	225	229	229	162	99	51	34
AT	–1.4	3	3.2	9.2	13.4	18.1	18.5	17.9	14.9	10.5	4.8	–0.4

Helsinki, Finland

DT: –18.5 deg   LAT: 60 deg 19'

	Jan	Feb	Mar	Apr	May	Jun	Jul	Aug	Sep	Oct	Nov	Dec
HDDC	812	725	672	459	264	75	53	87	225	375	534	703
HS	11	40	108	176	209	245	233	176	107	46	13	4
BSH	31	63	136	184	270	294	295	251	152	76	30	18
AT	–8.2	–7.9	–3.7	2.7	9.5	15.5	16.3	15.2	10.5	5.9	0.2	–4.7

Limoges, France

DT: –6.7 deg   LAT: 45 deg 49'

	Jan	Feb	Mar	Apr	May	Jun	Jul	Aug	Sep	Oct	Nov	Dec
HDDC	462	395	329	243	146	36	0	6	81	226	339	440
HS	48	81	130	175	219	250	237	199	150	100	52	35
BSH	75	96	151	188	207	225	240	221	185	154	84	59
AT	3.1	3.9	7.4	9.9	13.3	16.8	18.4	17.8	15.3	10.7	6.7	3.8

Nice, France

DT: 2.8 deg   LAT: 43 deg 42'

	Jan	Feb	Mar	Apr	May	Jun	Jul	Aug	Sep	Oct	Nov	Dec
HDDC	326	269	236	135	47	0	0	0	0	40	192	310
HS	72	102	163	223	254	283	297	247	191	136	83	67
BSH	148	165	196	243	272	312	363	324	263	200	155	137
AT	7.5	8.4	10.4	13.5	16.5	19.9	22.7	22.3	20.0	16.7	11.6	8.0

DT - outdoor winter design temperature (celsius)
HDDC - heating degree days (celsius)
HS - monthly average solar radiation on a horizontal surface (w/sq.m.)
BSH = # of bright sunshine hours (montly total)
AT - ambient temperature

Paris, France

DT: -3.9 deg   LAT: 48 deg 46'

	Jan	Feb	Mar	Apr	May	Jun	Jul	Aug	Sep	Oct	Nov	Dec
HDDC	450	367	409	291	105	0	0	0	24	189	264	456
HS	34	66	112	167	201	232	232	190	145	88	44	28
BSH	50	87	133	168	189	222	239	214	177	127	66	40
AT	3.5	4.9	4.8	8.3	14.6	19.1	18.1	18.9	17.2	11.9	9.2	3.3

Strasbourg, France

DT: -9.0 deg   LAT: 48 deg 35'

	Jan	Feb	Mar	Apr	May	Jun	Jul	Aug	Sep	Oct	Nov	Dec
HDDC	546	462	384	246	124	24	0	0	87	263	393	518
HS	39	70	119	168	213	228	221	185	137	90	40	29
BSH	49	68	148	188	211	206	225	216	168	121	49	36
AT	0.4	1.5	5.6	9.8	14.0	17.2	19.0	18.3	15.1	9.5	4.9	1.3

Shannon, Ireland

DT: -2.2 deg   LAT: 52 deg 40'

	Jan	Feb	Mar	Apr	May	Jun	Jul	Aug	Sep	Oct	Nov	Dec
HDDC	412	372	338	267	195	120	76	84	132	223	312	357
HS	30	60	110	174	202	238	211	173	131	73	41	24
BSH	43	76	115	153	167	174	152	146	123	84	66	40
AT	4.7	4.7	7.1	8.9	11.7	14.0	15.5	15.3	13.6	10.8	7.6	6.5

Milan, Italy

DT: -5.6 deg   LAT: 45 deg 26'

	Jan	Feb	Mar	Apr	May	Jun	Jul	Aug	Sep	Oct	Nov	Dec
HDDC	555	414	319	162	37	0	0	0	0	153	327	521
HS	40	77	136	203	243	276	288	238	173	111	50	37
BSH	53	84	155	186	211	240	285	236	174	143	66	50
AT	0.1	3.2	7.7	12.6	17.8	20.7	22.9	21.6	18.5	12.9	7.1	1.2

DT - outdoor winter design temperature (celsius)
HDDC - heating degree days (celsius)
HS - monthly average solar radiation on a horizontal surface (w/sq.m.)
BSH = # of bright sunshine hours (montly total)
AT - ambient temperature

Naples, Italy

DT: 2.2 deg   LAT: 40 deg 51'

	Jan	Feb	Mar	Apr	May	Jun	Jul	Aug	Sep	Oct	Nov	Dec
HDDC	322	269	239	135	31	0	0	0	0	50	153	279
HS	78	111	169	226	280	315	321	280	213	150	93	67
BSH	121	120	176	198	248	276	313	295	225	195	138	109
AT	7.6	8.4	10.3	13.5	17.0	20.7	23.1	22.9	20.3	16.4	12.9	9.0

Rome, Italy

DT: 0.6 deg   LAT: 41 deg 48'

	Jan	Feb	Mar	Apr	May	Jun	Jul	Aug	Sep	Oct	Nov	Dec
HDDC	347	280	248	138	31	0	0	0	0	60	165	310
HS	74	115	171	226	285	312	325	279	213	149	88	66
BSH	121	132	174	207	260	279	335	304	237	208	138	112
AT	6.8	8.0	10.0	13.4	17.1	21.1	23.9	12.7	20.7	15.1	12.5	8.0

Amsterdam, Netherlands

DT: -5.0 deg   LAT: 52 deg 06'

	Jan	Feb	Mar	Apr	May	Jun	Jul	Aug	Sep	Oct	Nov	Dec
HDDC	515	440	422	291	183	78	56	56	114	223	378	512
HS	25	53	94	149	195	218	194	179	123	72	33	21
BSH	40	64	109	153	192	210	192	204	141	102	54	43
AT	1.4	2.3	4.4	8.2	12.1	15.4	16.2	16.2	14.2	10.8	5.4	1.5

Oslo, Norway

DT: -15.7 deg   LAT: 59 deg. 56'

	Jan	Feb	Mar	Apr	May	Jun	Jul	Aug	Sep	Oct	Nov	Dec
HDDC	703	616	574	396	226	9	22	65	201	375	507	620
HS	13	36	92	141	210	205	192	145	88	55	16	8
BSH	47	92	159	170	216	234	221	172	132	87	46	24
AT	-4.7	-4	-0.5	4.8	10.7	14.7	17.3	15.9	11.3	5.9	1.1	-2.0

DT - outdoor winter design temperature (celsius)
HDDC - heating degree days (celsius)
HS - monthly average solar radiation on a horizontal surface (w/sq.m.)
BSH = # of bright sunshine hours (montly total)
AT - ambient temperature

Madrid, Spain

DT: -2.2 deg   LAT: 40 deg 25'

	Jan	Feb	Mar	Apr	May	Jun	Jul	Aug	Sep	Oct	Nov	Dec
HDDC	406	322	248	150	71	0	0	0	0	124	273	384
HS	61	93	126	175	225	267	271	212	151	85	50	44
BSH	153	173	187	235	279	317	382	352	256	206	157	136
AT	4.9	6.5	10.0	13.0	15.7	20.6	24.2	23.6	19.8	14.0	8.9	5.6

Stockholm, Sweden

DT: -13.4 deg   LAT: 59 deg 21'

	Jan	Feb	Mar	Apr	May	Jun	Jul	Aug	Sep	Oct	Nov	Dec
HDDC	679	627	570	405	251	57	40	62	171	310	474	617
HS	14	41	101	148	241	287	254	203	120	61	25	12
BSH	31	67	136	156	273	339	288	264	156	112	69	34
AT	-3.9	-4.4	-0.4	4.5	9.9	16.1	16.7	16.0	12.3	8.0	2.2	-1.9

Cambridge, U.K.

DT: -2.8 deg   LAT: 52 deg 12'

	Jan	Feb	Mar	Apr	May	Jun	Jul	Aug	Sep	Oct	Nov	Dec
HDDC	453	395	369	276	189	87	31	40.3	111	236	339	419
HS	29	49	95	139	188	215	189	158	119	57	34	25
BSH	53	70	118	153	192	201	186	177	138	105	57	40
AT	3.5	3.9	6.1	8.8	11.9	15.1	17.0	16.7	14.3	10.4	6.7	4.5

Eskdalemuir, U.K.

DT: -2.2 deg   LAT: 55 deg 19'

	Jan	Feb	Mar	Apr	May	Jun	Jul	Aug	Sep	Oct	Nov	Dec
HDDC	502	437	446	375	279	180	143	152	237	338	405	474
HS	16	47	84	135	162	195	169	143	96	54	27	14
BSH	28	67	96	135	149	177	146	136	96	74	54	37
AT	1.8	2.4	3.6	5.5	9.0	12.0	13.4	13.1	10.6	7.1	4.5	2.7

DT - outdoor winter design temperature (celsius)
HDDC - heating degree days (celsius)
HS - monthly average solar radiation on a horizontal surface (w/sq.m.)
BSH = # of bright sunshine hours (montly total)
AT - ambient temperature

London, U.K.

DT: -3.5 deg   LAT: 51 deg 31'

	Jan	Feb	Mar	Apr	May	Jun	Jul	Aug	Sep	Oct	Nov	Dec
HDDC	459	400	388	297	211	105	65	74	123	220	348	453
HS	23	46	86	127	172	208	183	151	113	65	34	20
BSH	40	70	18	141	195	225	195	183	147	105	69	43
AT	3.2	3.7	5.5	8.1	11.2	14.5	15.9	15.6	13.9	10.9	6.4	3.4

Hamburg, West Germany

DT: -9.0 deg   LAT: 53 deg 38'

	Jan	Feb	Mar	Apr	May	Jun	Jul	Aug	Sep	Oct	Nov	Dec
HDDC	567	487	468	315	198	63	56	62	126	248	393	552
HS	22	47	93	148	195	227	201	181	116	62	28	17
BSH	40	62	118	162	211	246	220	219	144	93	48	37
AT	-0.2	.6	2.9	7.5	11.6	15.9	16.2	16.0	13.8	10.0	4.9	0.2

Wurzburg, West Germany

DT: -11.8 deg   LAT: 49 deg 48'

	Jan	Feb	Mar	Apr	May	Jun	Jul	Aug	Sep	Oct	Nov	Dec
HDDC	595	498	440	288	149	54	0	28	129	301	429	552
HS	34	66	112	168	210	231	223	187	147	81	38	27
BSH	37	70	115	162	198	217	226	205	165	102	45	37
AT	-1.2	-0.2	3.8	8.4	13.2	16.6	18.2	17.1	13.7	8.3	3.8	0.2

Metric Conversion Table and Unit Abbreviations and Prefixes

Table F.1. Metric Conversion Table

Multiply	By	To Obtain
ft	0.3048	m
ft^2	0.0929	m^2
ft^3	0.0283	m^3
lb	0.454	kg
lb/ft^3	16.01	kg/m^3
gallon (IMP)	4.546	litre
gallon (US)	3.79	litre
litre	0.001	m^3
Btu/hr	0.2930	W
kWhr	3.6	MJ
J/sec	1	W
Btu/ft^2	1.135×10^4	J/m^2
$Btu/ft^2/day$	0.131	W/m^2
	0.0113	$MJ/m^2/day$
$R(ft^2 \cdot h°F/Btu)$	0.176	$RSI(m^2 \times °C/W)$
$U(Btuh/ft^2 \cdot °F)$	5.675	$W/m^2 \times °C$
MJ/day	11.57	W
PSI	6.894×10^3	P
deg. days (Fahrenheit)	5/9	deg. days (Celsius)

UNIT ABBREVIATIONS AND PREFIXES

m	milli	1 thousandth
c	centi	1 hundredth
k	kilo	1 thousand
M	mega	1 million
G	giga	1 billion (thousand million)
g	gram	
hr	hour	
J	Joule	
m	meter	
m^2	square meter	
m^3	cubic meter	
P	Pascal	
W	watt	

Sun Path Charts*

To determine the best location for a proposed building, it is desirable to plot the east–south–west skyline at the site. For the months of November to January it is particularly useful to know accurately how much direct sun will reach the site. "Plotting the skyline" consists of using a compass, protractor, or clinometer to record the altitude and azimuth angles of all natural landscape, trees, and buildings that will block winter sun, and superimposing the plotted skyline on the sun chart for the latitude nearest to that of the location. Charts are given for north latitudes 28° to 56°.

EXAMPLE

To plot the skyline proceed as follows:

1. With the compass locate 0° azimuth, that is, true south.
2. Determine the altitude, or degrees above the horizon, of true south and mark this point above 0° (S) on the chart.
3. Proceed eastward and then westward and record the altitudes of the skyline every 15° (azimuth) or so. Detail the outline of any high-rise buildings or tall coniferous trees, and so forth. Note accurately the azimuth and altitude of these objects.
4. Sketch the outline of deciduous trees, keeping in mind that in the winter most direct sun will manage to shine through the branches of these trees.
5. Connect the plotted points, as in the example chart. (Dotted lines indicate deciduous trees.) The areas above the line will give the hours in the day when direct sun will reach the site.

Note that the times given on the charts are solar time. Conversion to clock time is easily achieved with reference to any astronomy handbook, but is not necessary for determination of effective sunshine hours.

---

*The sun path charts are from Mazria, Edward, *The Passive Solar Energy Book*. Rodale Press, Emmaus, PA, 1979. Copyright © 1979. Reprinted with permission of Rodale Press, Inc.

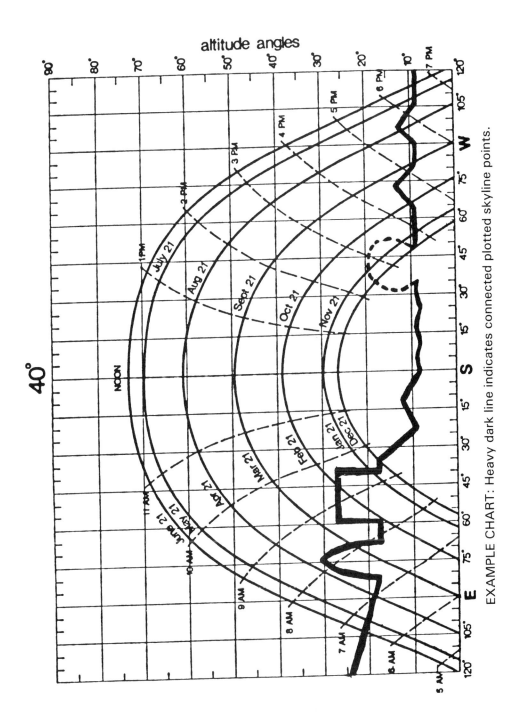

EXAMPLE CHART: Heavy dark line indicates connected plotted skyline points.

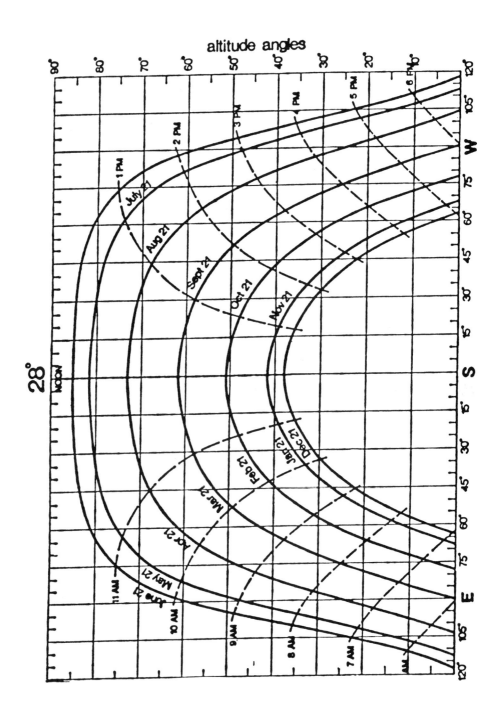

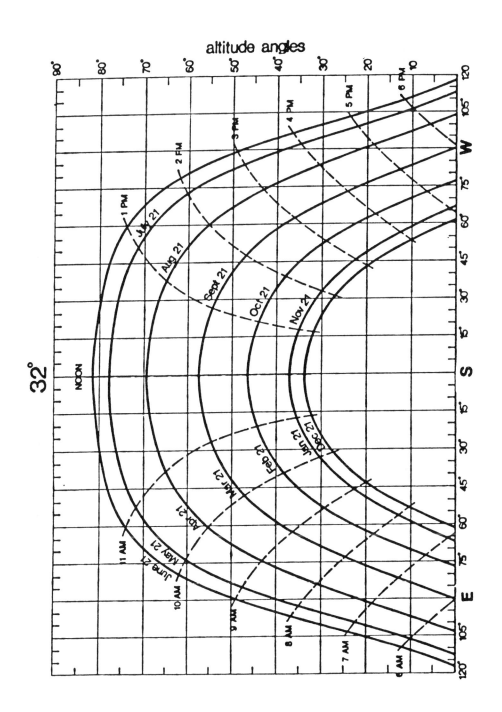

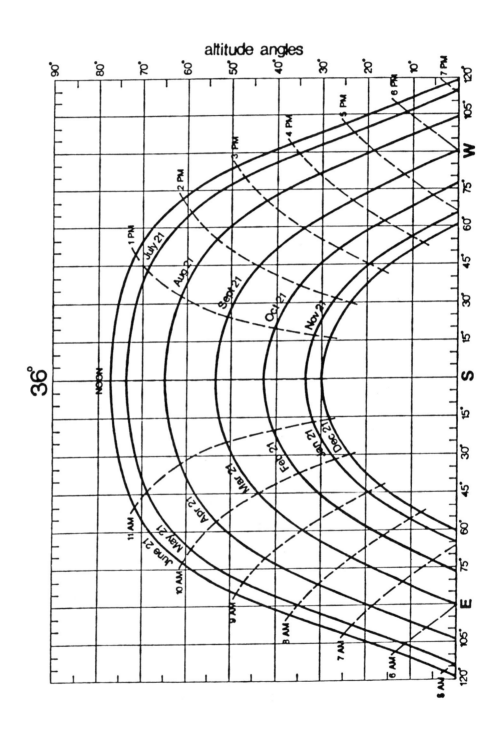

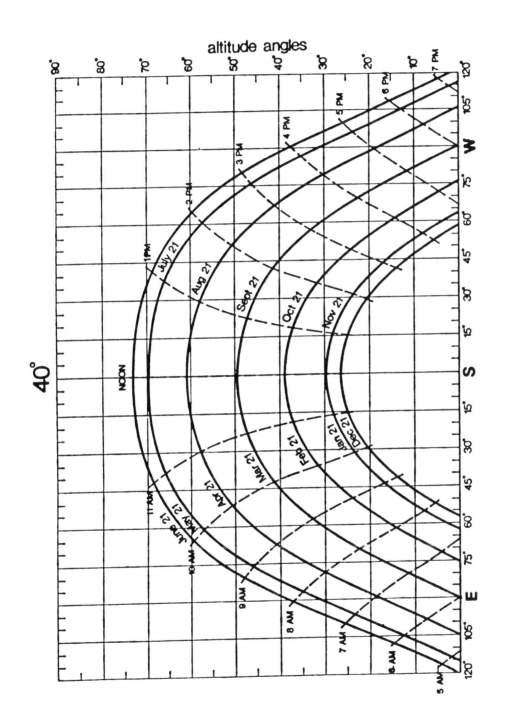

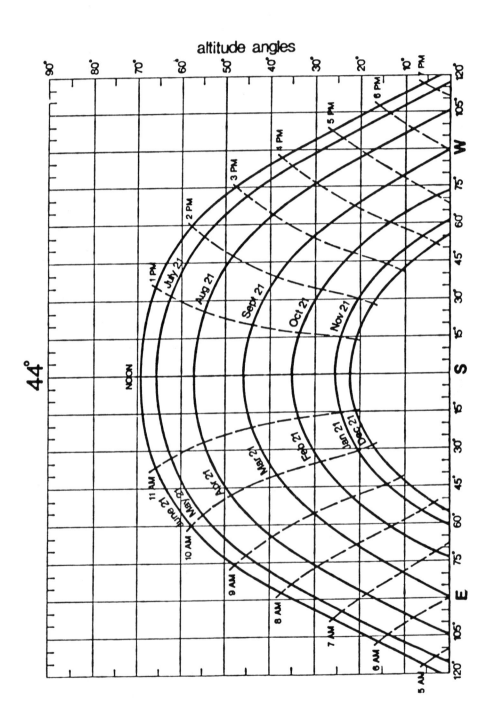

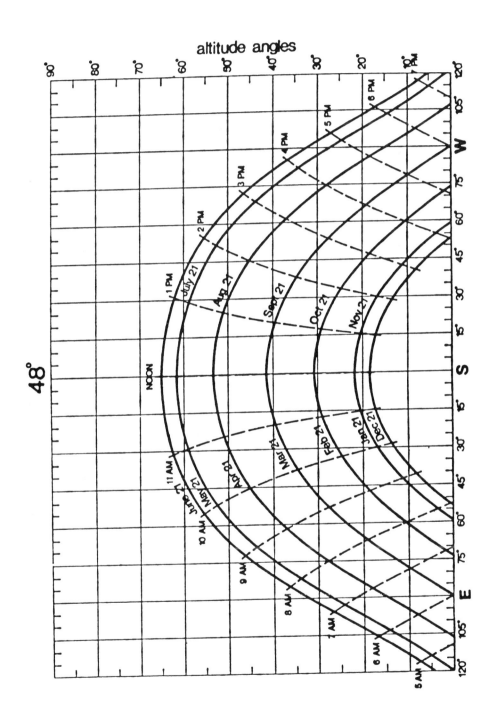

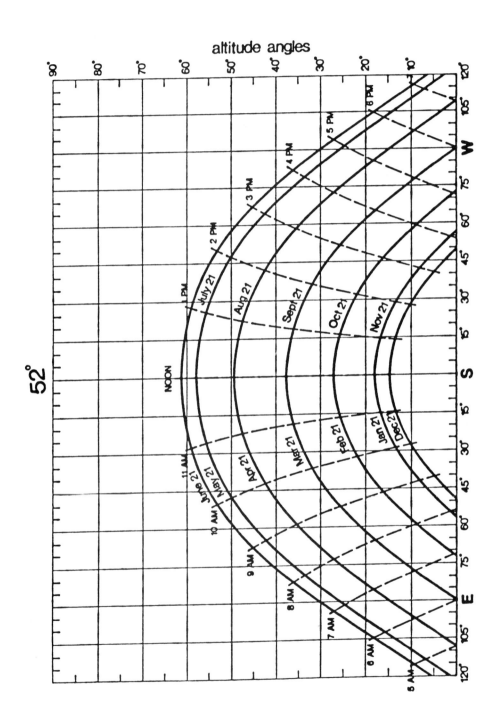

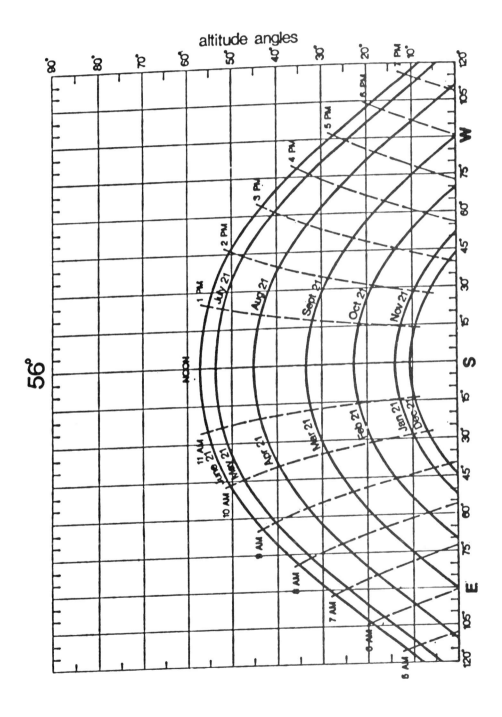

Glossary

Italicized terms are defined in the glossary.

Active solar – The utilization of solar energy in conjunction with other systems or mechanical devices, as in a solar collector.

Albedo – The fraction of sunlight striking a surface that is reflected back up again. It varies widely from zero up to about 0.5 for a surface covered with fresh snow.

Arcs – Components of a *heat transfer network* joining the nodes, and to which *thermal transmittances* are assigned. Physically, the arcs often represent boundaries such as walls and roofs, or the transfer of heated air by a fan.

Conduction – Heat transfer due to the transfer of kinetic energy between neighbouring molecules. In a solid, this is the vibrational energy of fixed molecules and is the dominant effect. In a gas, it occurs in molecular collisions and is for the purposes of this book negligible.

Convection – Heat transfer that occurs when fluids are set in motion due to internal temperature differences. It is important when heat is transported to and from surfaces such as walls and windows, and in the air spaces between surfaces.

Design temperature – The normal low winter temperature. The outdoor temperature is beneath this temperature a certain percentage of the time. The design temperature used in the book is the 1% design temperature, but 5% is also common.

Differential equations – Equations that include rates of change (derivatives) and/or the rates of change of derivatives, and so on, of a variable. It is necessary to solve for the variable itself, which in the equations describing a thermal network is temperature.

Eigenvalues, eigenvectors – Literally, the proper values and vectors of a matrix, used in solving systems of *differential equations*, and in many other applications. We refer the reader to any introductory text in linear algebra.

Finite difference solution – This is an important method for solving *differential equations* on a computer, whereby the continuous time variation in the differential equations is approximated by a number of discrete time steps. In some cases the time step used must be very small to give an accurate solution.

Heat capacity – See *Thermal capacity*.

164

Heat transfer coefficient — The value representing the *thermal transmittance* between two zones, which is arrived at by totaling the transmittances of all the common boundaries between the two zones.

Internal gain — Heat gain to a building zone due to people, animals, appliances, and other internal sources.

Iterative methods — The solution of mathematical equations by means of successive approximations.

Linear heat transfer model — A model in which the rate of heat transfer is approximated by a constant times temperature difference. Because all the parameters in this equation occur to the first power, its graph makes a straight line — thus "linear."

Matrix — A two-dimensional array of numbers, which commonly relates one *vector* to another vector. Thus, for example, the heat transfer matrix in a network relates the temperature vector to the heat flow vector. See any introductory text on linear algebra.

Modes — The decaying transient terms in the solution to equations by the modal or spectral method. See chapter 10.

Nodes — Components of a *heat transfer network model* representing building zones or structural materials, to which thermal mass, heat sources, and temperatures are allocated.

Passive solar — The utilization of solar energy for heating and cooling through the layout, orientation, and design of the building, rather than attached machinery.

Radiation — See *Thermal radiation*.

Resistance — See *Thermal resistance*.

Solar gain — The solar radiation entering a building zone that is converted into heat energy upon striking a surface.

Solar transmittance, transmissivity — The proportion of solar radiation that passes through a material, such as a window.

Specific heat — The amount of heat required to raise the temperature of a unit mass of a material 1°C (or given off in a 1°C fall).

Steady-state heat transfer model — A heat-transfer model in which temperature does not vary with time. It is much simpler computationally than a nonsteady-state model, but does not allow for any time variations. As explained in the text, however, a steady-state model can be used to compute average temperatures and heat flows over a cycle.

Thermal capacity — The amount of heat required to raise the temperature of a unit volume of a material 1°C (or given off in a 1°C fall). Also called the *volume specific heat*.

Thermal conductance — The thermal transmittance of a conducting solid, often used interchangeably with thermal transmittance.

Thermal mass (C) — The amount of heat required to raise the temperature of a building component 1°C (or given off in a 1°C fall). It is the *thermal capacity* times the volume of the component, or the *specific heat* times its mass.

Thermal network — A model of a building in which the building zones and any important structures are represented by *nodes* and separated by *arcs*, representing walls, heat transfer by ventilation, etc.

Thermal radiation — The transfer of energy in the form of electromagnetic waves that are emitted in proportion to the fourth power of the temperature of a surface. For hot objects such as the sun, most of the radiation is visible, but for everyday objects it is in the infrared range of the spectrum.

Thermal resistance (R) – The inverse of *thermal transmittance*, and a measure of the resistance of a material to the flow of heat.

Thermal transmittance (U) – The amount of heat flow through a structure per degree Centigrade temperature difference across it. It is the inverse of the *thermal resistance*, and a measure of the ease with which heat flows. See also *Heat transfer coefficient*.

Time constants – The time it takes for the exponent of a *mode* to equal -1, indicating that mode has decayed to about one-third of its initial value. It is the inverse of the *eigenvalue* corresponding to that mode.

Transmittance – Refer to either *Thermal transmittance* or *Solar transmittance*, as the case may be.

Vector – A set of quantities in the form $(a, b, c, \ldots, n)$ representing values of some parameter in different places, times, directions, etc. In the linear heat transfer model, the temperature and heat source vectors have as components the values of these variables at the various nodes.

Vector equation – In an equation involving vectors, the values of each component are equated, giving a system of equations. The equation resulting from the linear heat transfer network model is such an equation.

Bibliography

GENERAL SOLAR ENERGY

Alves, Ronald and Charles Milligan, *Living with Energy*. Penguin, New York, 1978.

Butti, Ken and John Perlin, *A Golden Thread, 2500 Years of Solar Architecture and Technology*. Cheshire, Palo Alto, CA, 1980.

Cole, John N., *Sun Reflections*. Rodale, Emmaus, PA, 1981.

Daniels, Farrington, *Direct Use of the Sun's Energy*. Yale University Press, New Haven, CT, 1964.

Halacy, D. S., Jr., *The Coming Age of Solar Energy*, Revised ed. Harper and Row, New York, 1973.

Hawkes, Jacquetta, *Man and the Sun*. Cresset, London, 1962.

Herdeg, Walter (Ed.), *The Sun in Art*. Amstutz and Herdeg, Graphis, Zurich, 1962.

McDaniels, David K., *The Sun: Our Future Energy Source*. Wiley, New York, 1979.

Messel, H. and S. T. Butler, *Solar Energy*. Pergamon, Oxford, 1975.

SOLAR BUILDINGS

Anderson, Bruce and Michael Riordan, *The Solar Home Book*. Cheshire, Harrisville, NH, 1976.

Argue, Robert, *The Well-Tempered House, Energy-Efficient Building for Cold Climates*. Renewable Energy in Canada, Toronto, 1980.

Bainbridge, David, Judy Corbett, and John Hofacre, *Village Home's Solar House Designs*. Rodale, Emmaus, PA, 1979.

Carriere, Dean and Fraser Day, *Solar Houses for a Cold Climate*. Wiley, Toronto, 1980.

Charters, W. W. S., Twenty centuries of solar design. *Sunworld* 7, 56–57 (1983).

Eccli, Eugene (Ed.), *Low-Cost Energy-Efficient Shelter*. Rodale, Emmaus, PA, 1976.

Gough, Bruce D., Passive Solar Heating in Canada (Report ER 79-6). Energy, Mines and Resources Canada, Ottawa, 1979.

Kadulksi, Richard and Terry Lyster, *SOLPLAN 5, Energy Conserving Passive Solar Houses for Canada*. Drawing Room Graphics, Vancouver, 1981.

Mazria, Edward, *The Passive Solar Energy Book*. Rodale, Emmaus, PA, 1979.

McHarg, Ian L., *Design with Nature*. Doubleday, New York, 1971.

McKown, Cora, *Passive and Low Energy Alternatives*. Pergamon, Elmsford, NY, 1982.

Stein, Richard G., *Architecture and Energy*. Anchor/Doubleday, New York, 1977.
U.S. Government Department of Housing and Urban Development, *Solar Dwelling Designs*. Sterling, New York, 1980.
Wade, Alex and Neal Ewenstein, *30 Energy-Efficient Houses*. Rodale, Emmaus, PA, 1977.

CHAPTERS 1–3. CLIMATE, SITE, CONSTRUCTION

Argue, Robert and Brian Marshall, *The Superinsulated Retrofit Book*. Renewable Energy in Canada, Toronto, 1981.
Olgyay, V. V., *Design with Climate*. Princeton University Press, Princeton, NJ, 1963.
Ontario Ministry of Energy, *Subdivisions and Sun*. Government of Ontario, Toronto, 1979.
Robinette, C. *et al., Landscape Planning for Energy Conservation*. Environmental Design Press, 1977.
Watson, Donald and Kenneth Labs, *Climatic Design—Energy-Efficient Building Principles and Practices*. McGraw-Hill, New York, 1983.

CHAPTER 4. SPECIAL PASSIVE TYPES

McCullagh, James C. (Ed.), *The Solar Greenhouse Book*. Rodale, Emmaus, PA, 1978.
Shurcliff, William A., *Superinsulated Houses and Double Envelope Houses*. Brick House, Andover, MA, 1981.
Shurcliff, William A., *Super Solar Houses, Saunders' 100% Solar, Low-Cost Designs*. Brick House, Andover, MA, 1983.
Underground Space Center, University of Minnesota, *Earth Sheltered Housing Design*. Van Nostrand Reinhold, New York, 1979.
Woods, Charles, *Natural Architecture, 4, Earth Sheltered Designs*. Van Nostrand Reinhold, New York, 1984.

CHAPTERS 5 AND 6. GLASS AND MASS

Evans, Ben, *Daylighting in Architecture*. McGraw-Hill, New York, 1981.
Langdon, William K., *Movable Insulation*. Rodale, Emmaus, PA, 1980.
Reale, F., Materials in solar energy systems (Vol. 3, pp. 1858–1874). *Solar World Congress*. Pergamon, Elmsford, NY, 1984.
Shurcliff, William A., *Thermal Shutters and Shades*. Brick House, Andover, MA, 1980.

PART 2: QUANTITATIVE DESIGN

American Society of Heating, Refrigerating, and Airconditioning Engineers, *Handbook of Fundamentals*. Author, New York, 1981.
Balcomb, J. Douglas (Ed.), *Passive Solar Design Handbook* (Vol. 2). U.S. Department of Energy, Washington, DC, 1980.
Cowan, H. J. (Ed.), *Predictive Methods for the Energy Conserving Design of Buildings*. Pergamon, Sydney, Australia, 1983.
Dumont, R. S., M. E. Lux, and H. W. Orr, *HOTCAN: A Computer Program for Estimating the Space Heating Requirement of Residences (CP49)*. National Research Council of Canada, Ottawa, 1982.
Iqbal, M., *An Introduction to Solar Radiation*. Academic, New York, 1983.
Jones, Robert W. (Ed.), *Passive Solar Design Handbook*. American Solar Energy Society, New York, 1983.
Lebens, Ralph M., *Passive Solar Heating Design*. Wiley, New York, 1980.
Los Alamos National Laboratory, Heat Storage and Distribution Inside Buildings (Report LA-9694-MS), 1983.
McFarland, R. D., PASOLE: A General Simulation Program for Passive Solar Energy (Los Alamos National Laboratory, Report LA-7433-MS), 1978.
Ontario Ministry of Energy, *Residential Passive Solar Heating, Review and Development of Design Aids*. Government of Ontario, Toronto, 1980.

APPENDIX B. MATHEMATICS

Carslaw, H. S. and J. C. Jaegar, *Conduction of Heat in Solids* (2nd ed.). Clarendon, Oxford, 1965.

Carter, C., *Predicting Passive Solar Performance Using Modal Expansions* (pp. 309–313). 3rd U.S. National Passive Solar Conference, San Jose, CA. American Section, International Solar Energy Society, Boulder, CO, 1979.

Carter, C., *Solving the Heat Transfer Network Equations in Passive Solar Simulations* (pp. 238–242). 5th U.S. National Passive Solar Conference, Amherst, MA. American Section, International Solar Energy Society, Boulder, CO, 1980.

Index

About the Authors

Cyril Carter is Chairman of the Environmental and Resource Studies Program and Professor of Mathematics at Trent University, Peterborough, Canada. Dr. Carter completed his Ph.D. at University College, London, England. He has published some 30 papers in the application of mathematics to a variety of energy problems. Dr. Carter worked for 6 years on nuclear reactor theory at Harwell, then for 6 years on magnetohydrodynamic electricity generation. Since 1976 he has been working on the computer simulation of passive solar buildings. He is currently a director of the Solar Energy Society of Canada.

Johan de Villiers is an architect in private practice in Peterborough, Canada. He was educated and trained in Pretoria, South Africa. His office has practiced on four continents, including such prestigious projects as Toronto's Eaton Centre and First Canadian Place. He has recently completed a lakeside condominium development with many passive solar features in Bobcaygeon, Canada. He is joint author with Cyril Carter of a paper on microcomputer passive solar simulation at the 1983 International Solar Energy Society meeting in Perth, Australia.